Published by ©Piano Notion
1st edition 2019 / revised 2022
www.pianonotion.com

Author: Bobby Cyr

Graphic design: Imagine Design

Logo: Studio Azura

Revision and communication: Marie-France Palardy

Translation: Traductions Kaizen

U.K revision: Ellie Jaggers and Emma Palmer

Legal deposit: Bibliothèque nationale du Québec, 2022

Legal deposit: Library and Archives Canada, 2022

ISMN: 979-0-9001551-0-8

Presentation

This piano method contains a collection of pieces and may also be used as a repertoire book. The method gives students the opportunity to build on prior learning and fully assimilate the material as the pieces become increasingly difficult.

Musical concepts are presented one at a time, with examples and exercises provided in the Appendices. Students then put these new concepts into practice as they learn and perform the pieces, further exploring and assimilating the new ideas and skills.

Book three builds a stronger understanding of accompaniment. Arpeggios will be studied separately in a number of pieces. Although this book can be used as a repertoire book, we recommend that you review the preceding books in the series in order to ensure a solid understanding of the musical concepts required for these pieces.

The repertoire

The repertoire was carefully selected from among the most beautiful songs from around the world. The date of composition as well as the country of origin of each song is indicated along with the title. The composer's name is also given, and if the composer is unknown, a Roud number is provided. The Roud Folk Song Index is a database of songs collected from oral tradition from all over the world.

Music reading exercises

To further develop your music reading skills, an exercise with syncopated rhythms is provided in the appendix.

Copyright and intellectual property

For more information, visit: www.pianonotion.com

Table of Contents

Level 11 pieces

Left hand arpeggios

The arpeggio is one of the most common piano accompaniments.
Chords and arpeggios are made up of the same notes.
Arpeggios are played with a specific fingering that allows the hand to move up and down the keyboard in order to play several octaves.
In this book, arpeggios are introduced one at a time in different musical contexts.

Chords and arpeggiated chords

Chords and arpeggiated chords are played with the same fingering.

C major chord Arpeggiated C major chord

Arpeggios

An arpeggio is made up of the same notes but is played with a different fingering.

C arpeggio

The thumb serves as a pivot point to help the hand move up and down the keyboard to reach several octaves.

The two-octave C arpeggio

Fifths and octaves

Before learning arpeggios, it is important to master fifths and octaves.
Fifths and octaves are the foundation of all major and minor arpeggios.
Sometimes the sustain pedal is used while playing arpeggios. Make sure you release the pedal when you change arpeggios so that the sound doesn't become muddy.

Exercise: Play a fifth followed by an octave in the left hand.

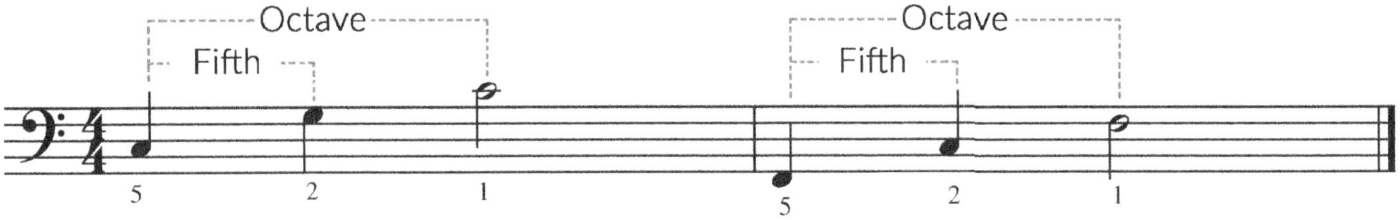

Octave
Fifth
Octave
Fifth

The Water Is Wide

Scotland (1904)

Unknown composer
Roud 87
Arr. Bobby Cyr

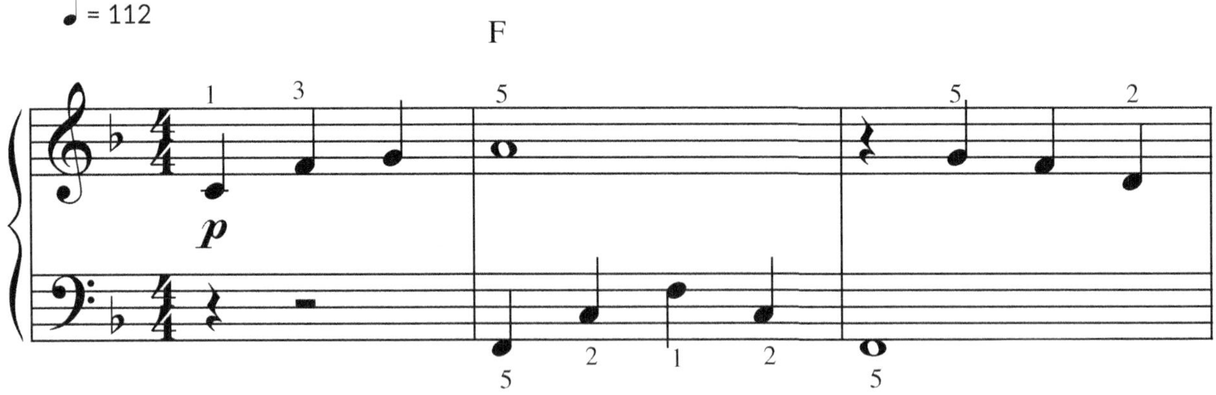

♩ = 112

F

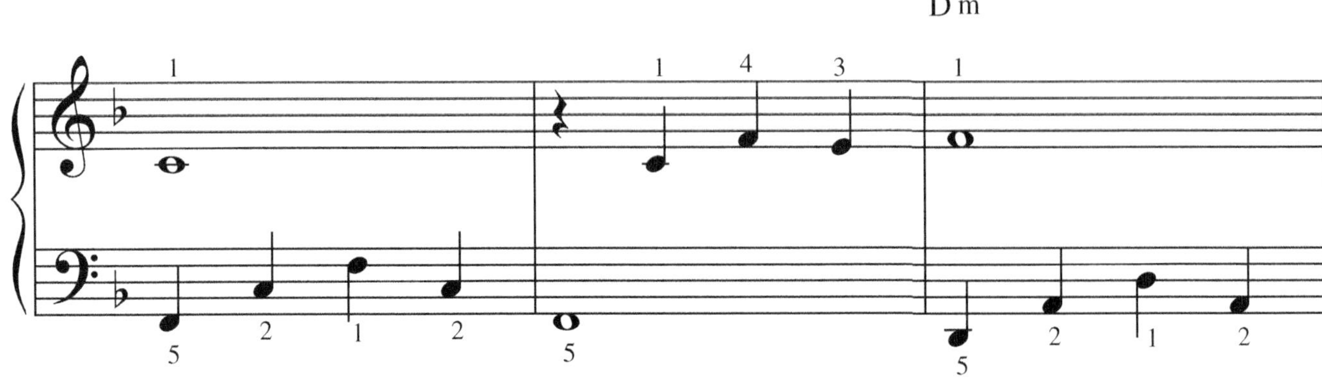

The Water Is Wide

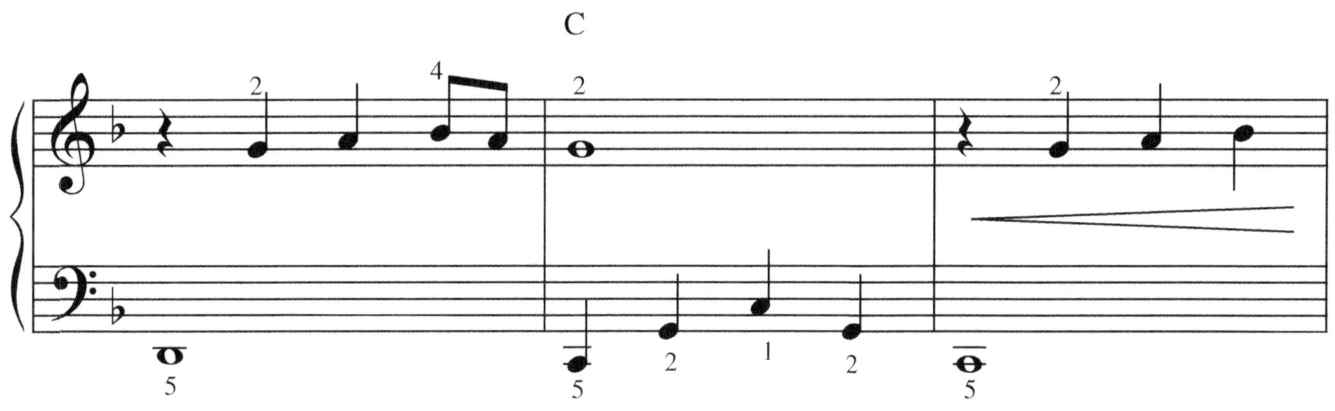

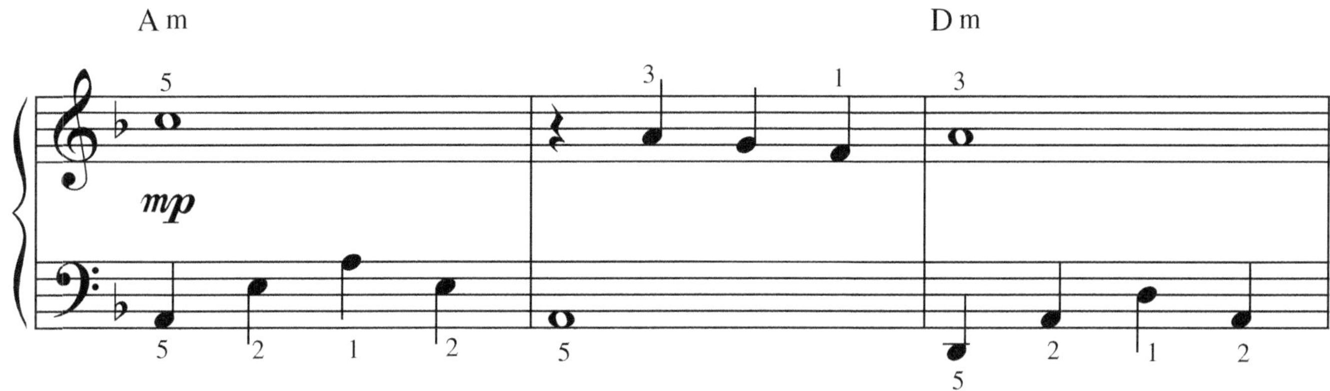

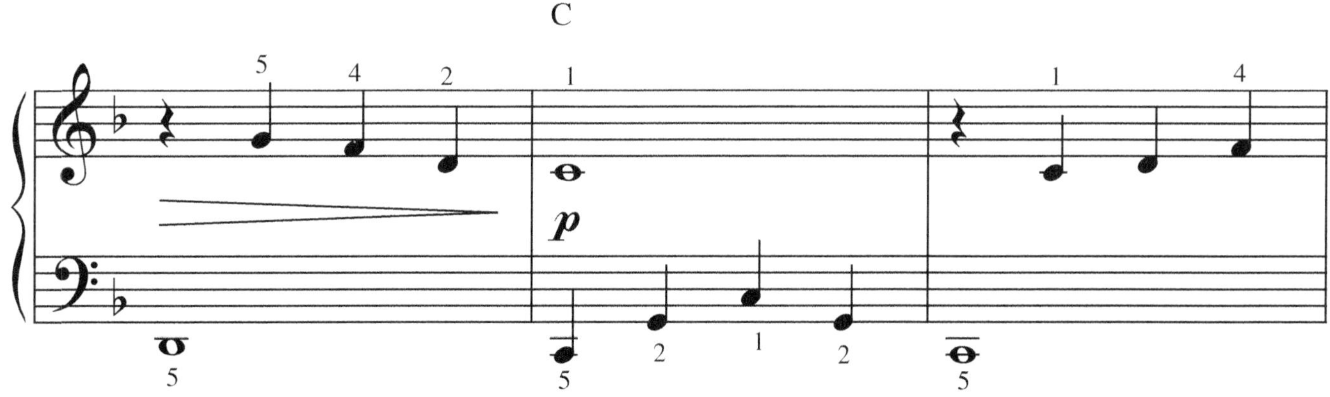

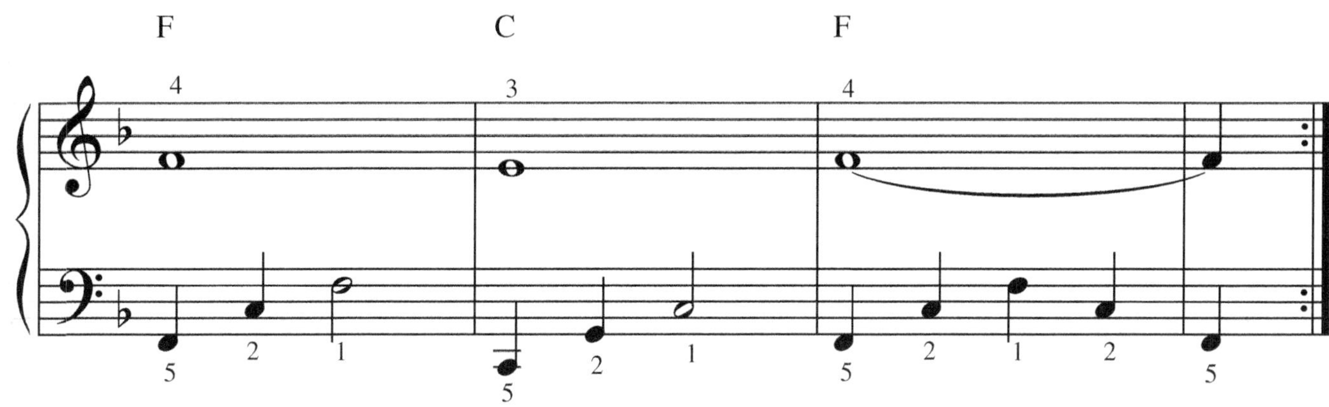

Down By The Salley Gardens

Ireland (1889)

Unknown composer
Arr. Bobby Cyr

♩ = 80

G D C G

mp

C D G

G D C G

C D G

mf

Down By The Salley Gardens

When Johnny Comes Marching Home

United States (1863)

Thomas Brigham Bishop
(1835-1905)
Arr. Bobby Cyr

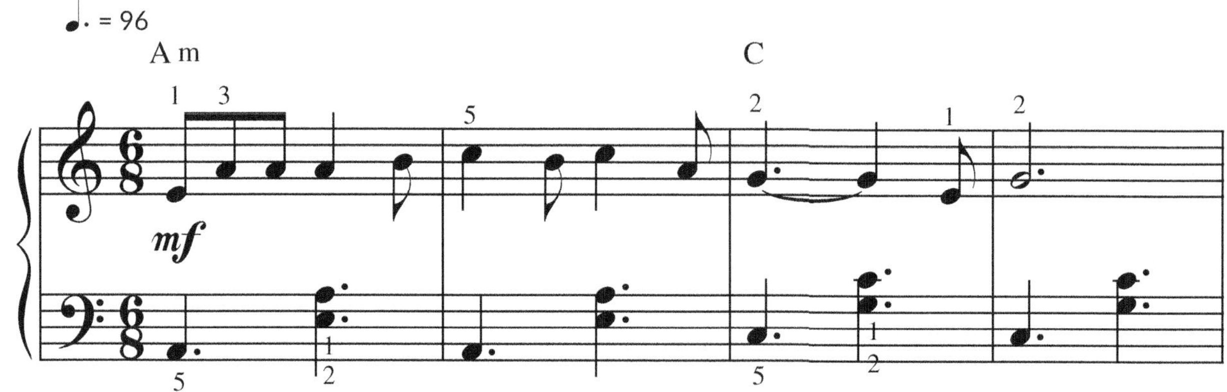

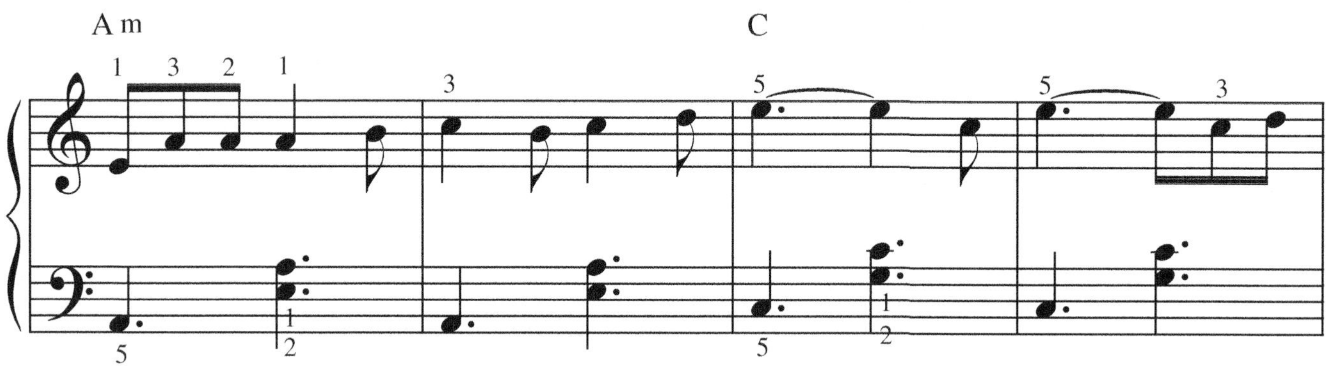

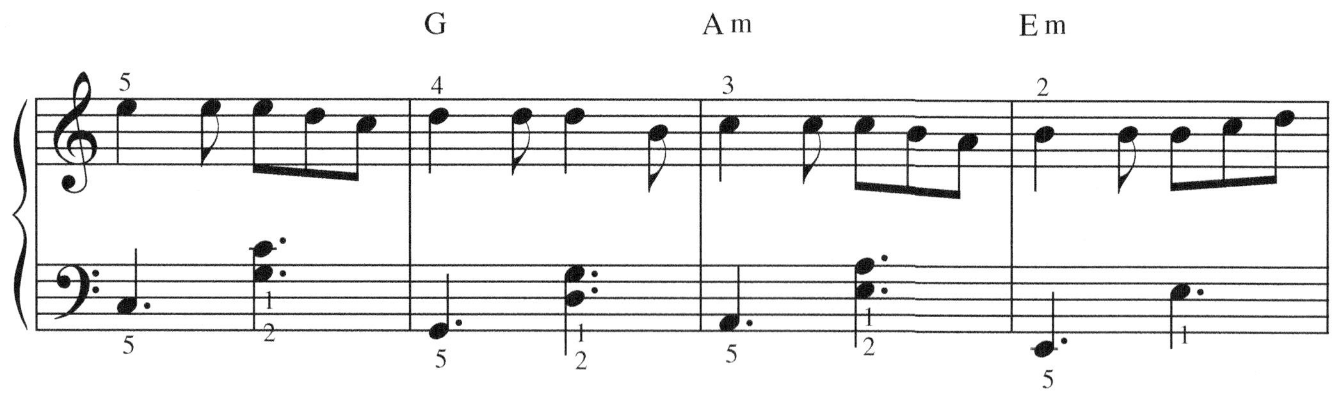

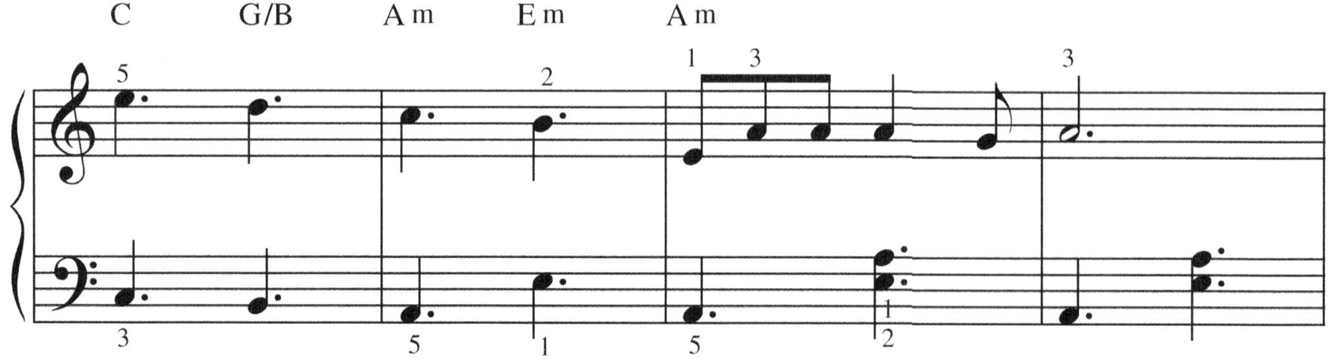

When Johnny Comes Marching Home

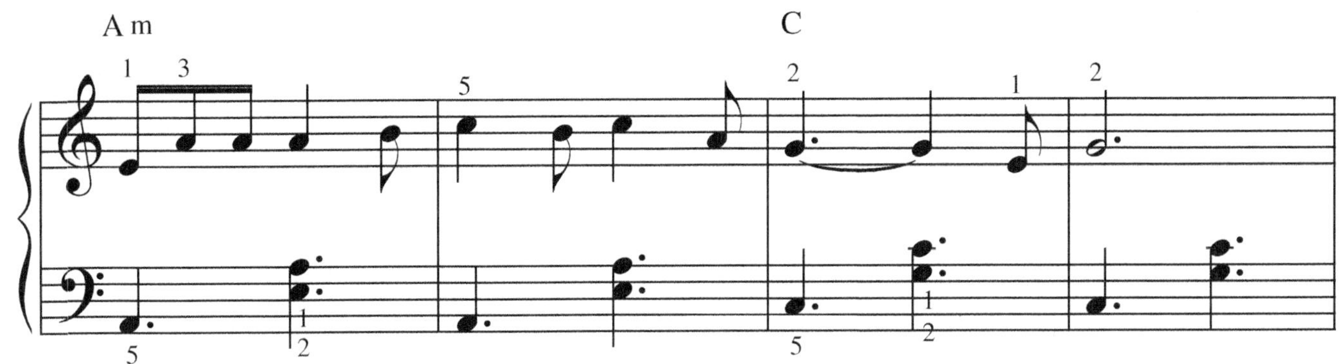

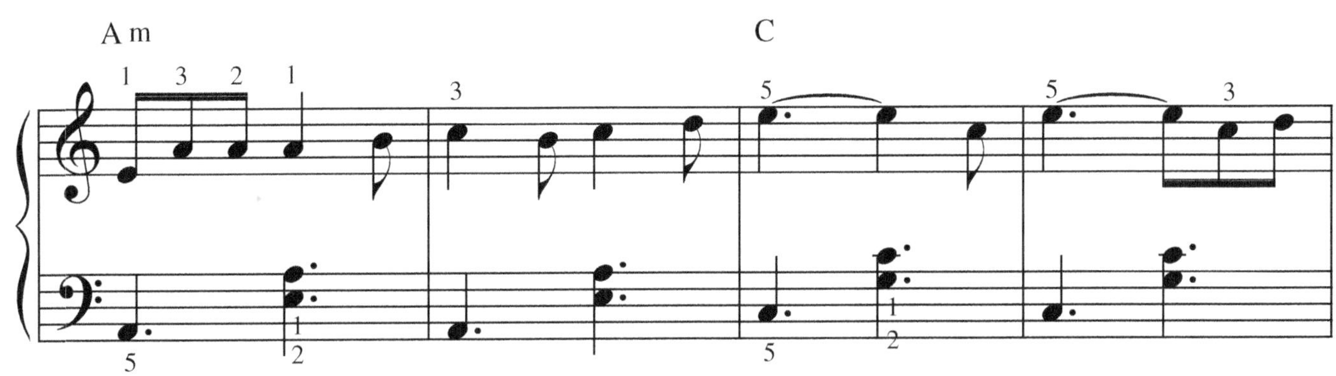

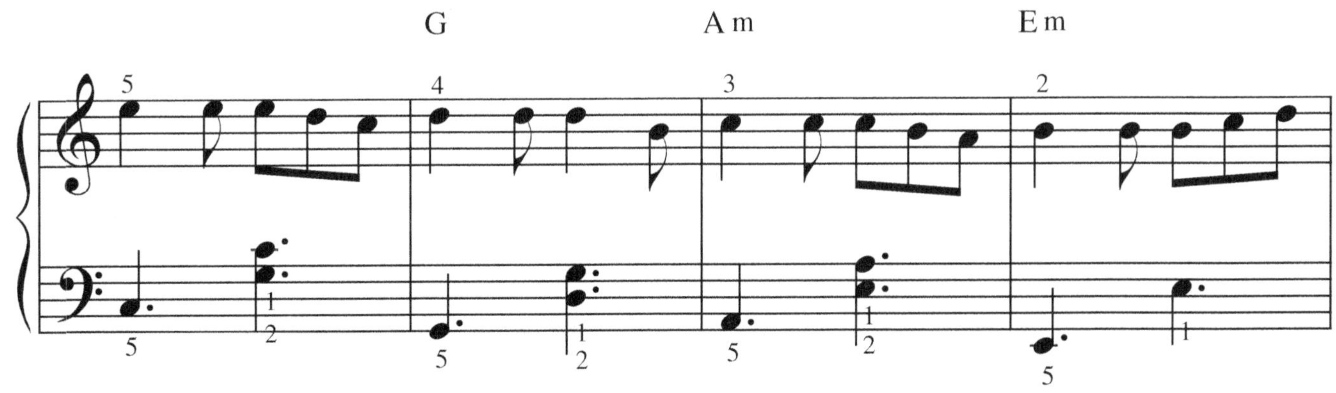

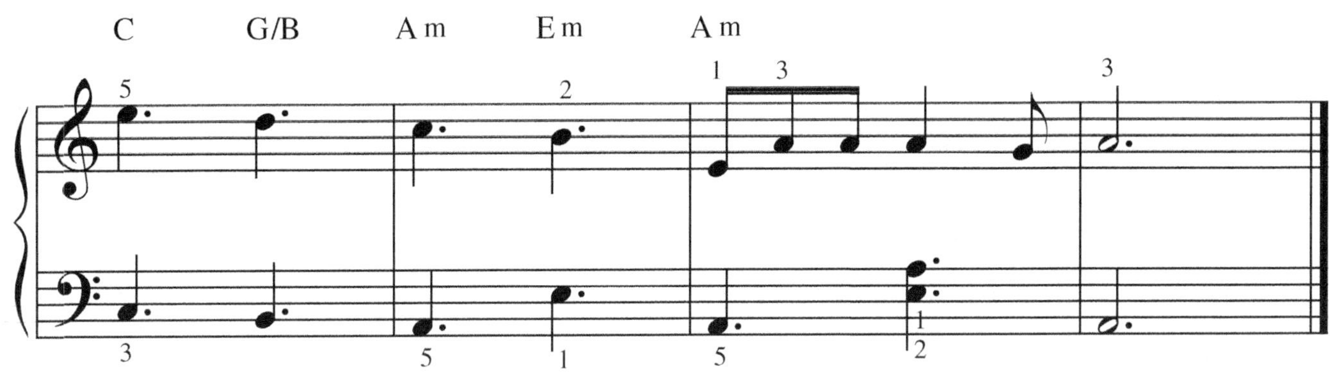

Auld Lang Syne

Scotland (1711)

Robert Burns
(1759-1796)
Arr. Bobby Cyr

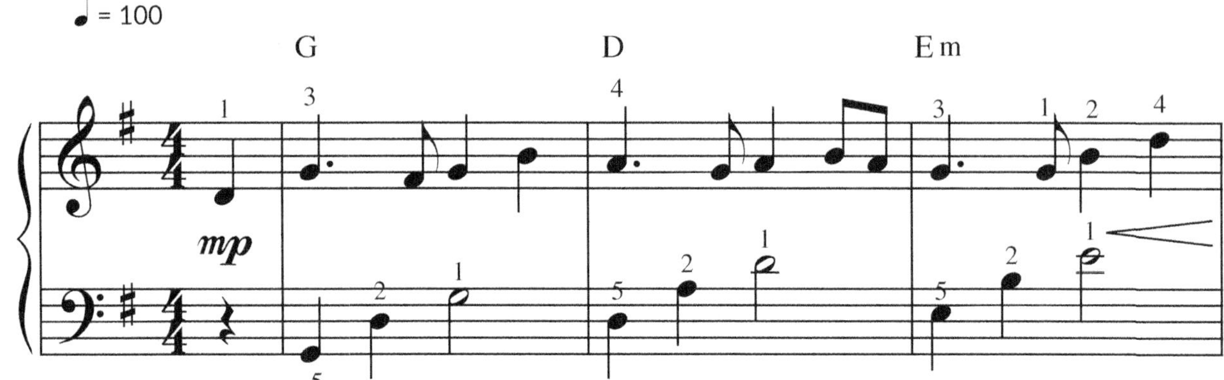

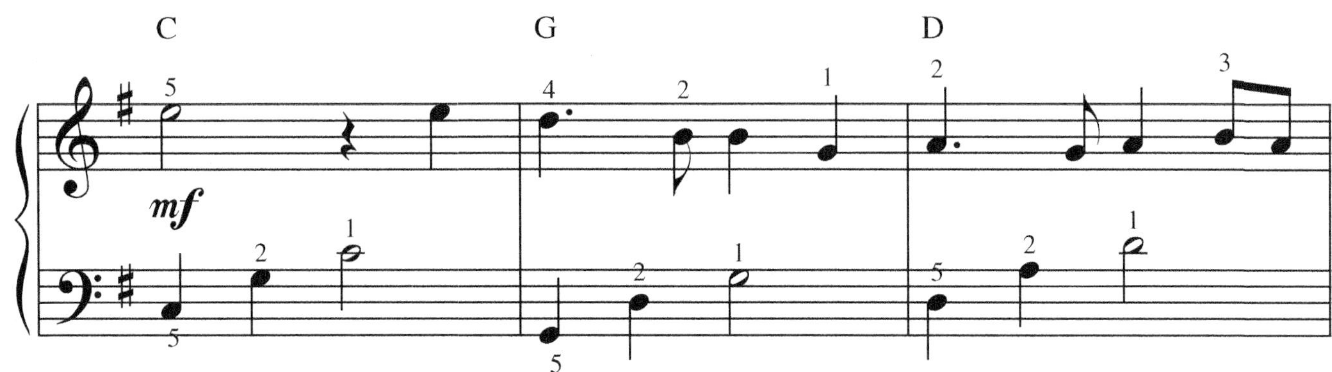

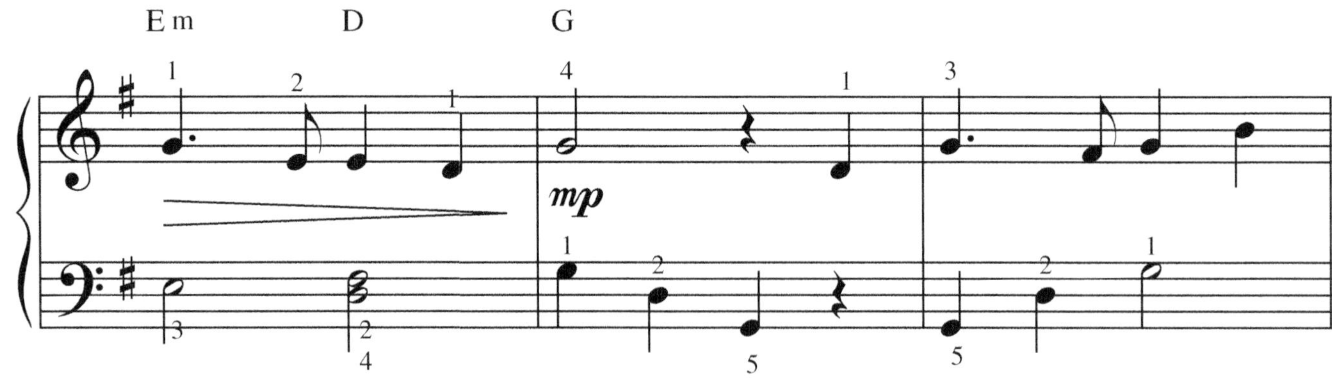

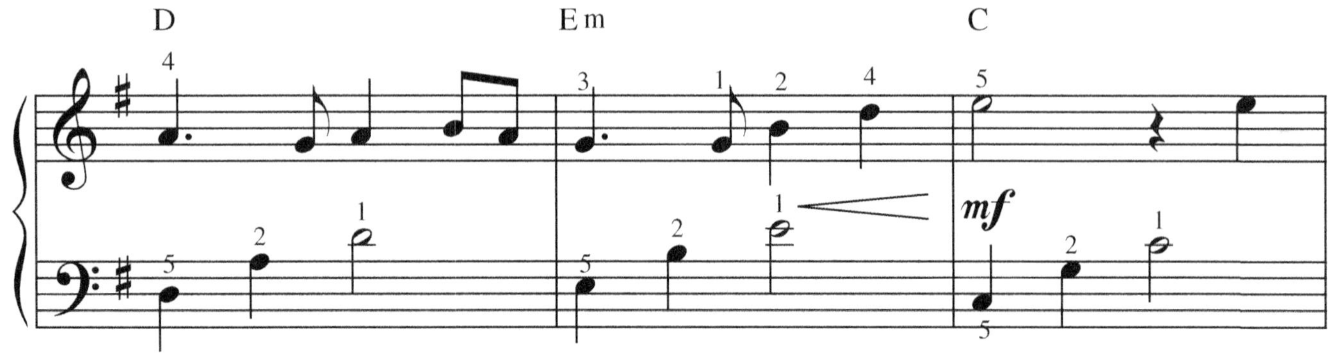

Auld Lang Syne

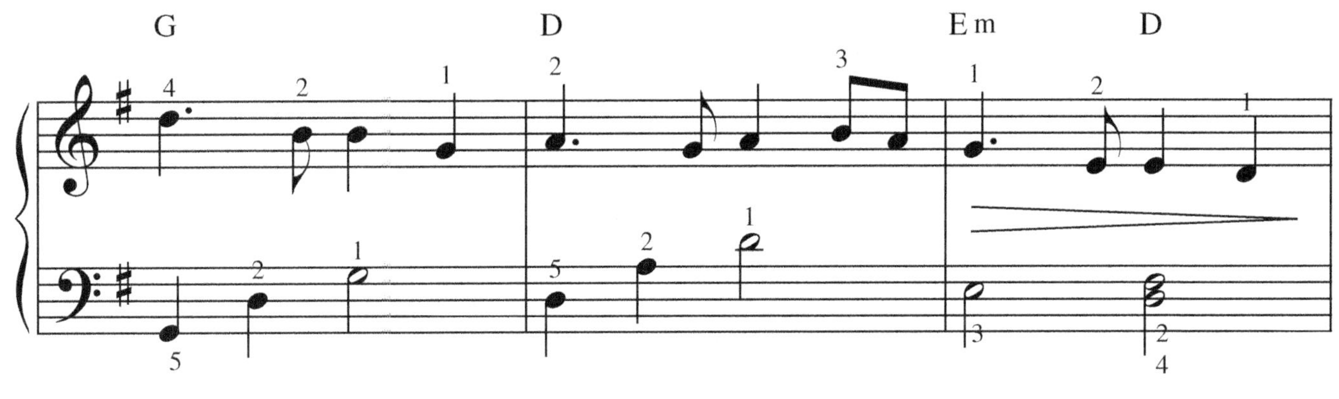

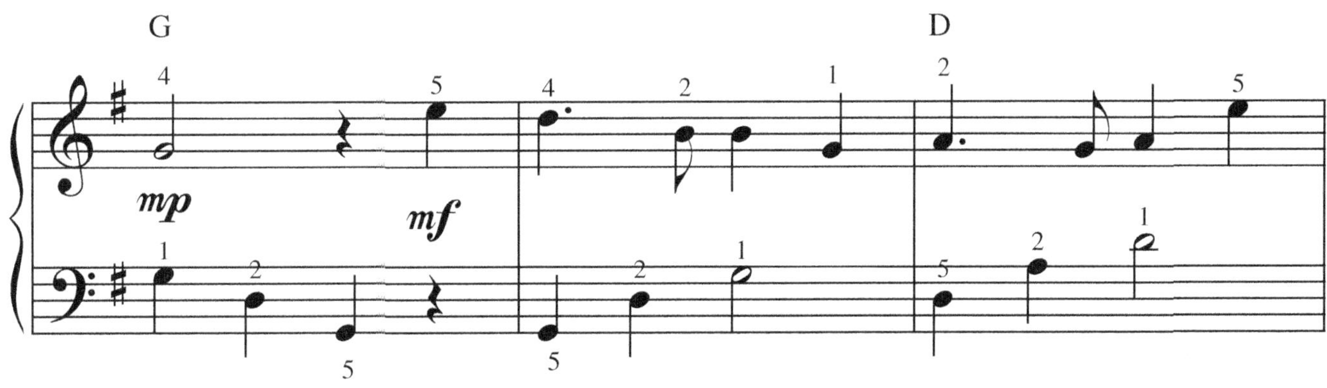

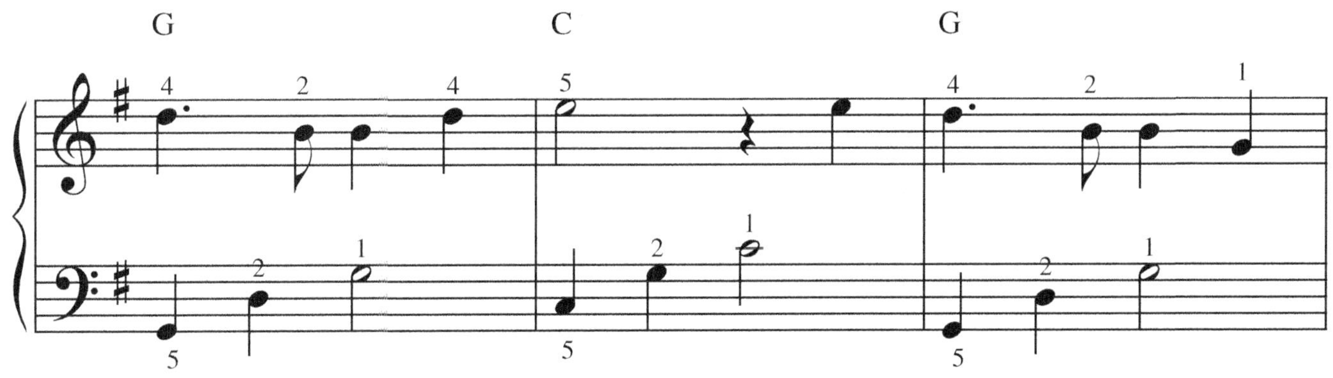

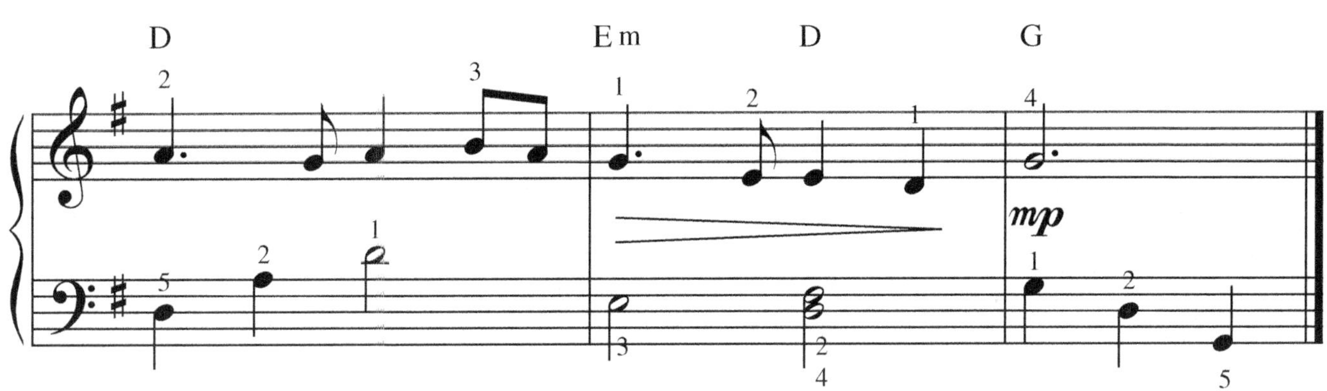

Arpeggios with thirds played on white keys

An arpeggio may span more than one octave.
Playing the third an octave higher adds more colour to the arpeggio.
Cross your second finger (L.H.2) over your thumb to play the third with the left hand.

Exercise: Play the following arpeggios with the left hand.

C (root position) C (with the third played an octave higher)

Down in the Valley

United States (1910)

Unknown composer
Roud 943
Arr. Bobby Cyr

♩. = 66

F

mp

Down in the Valley

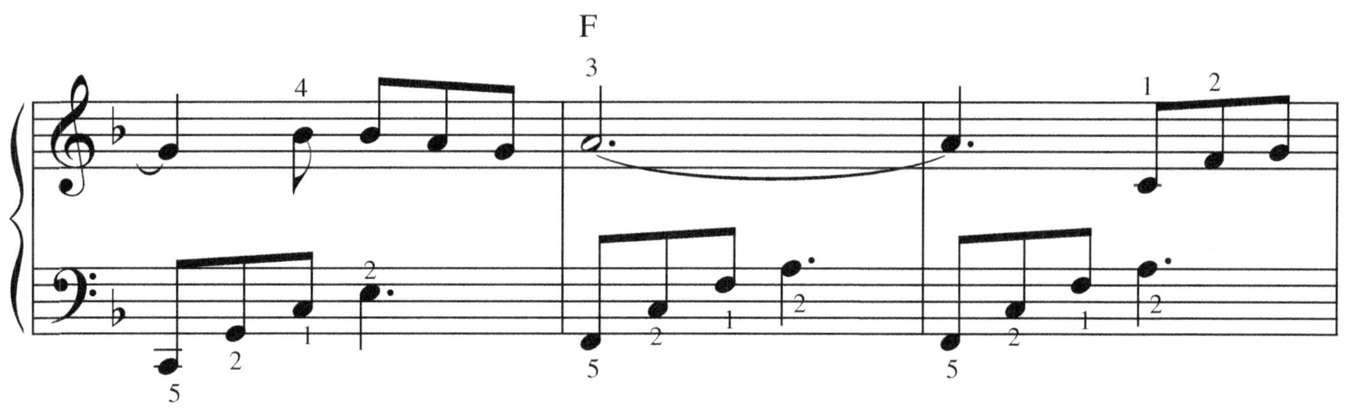

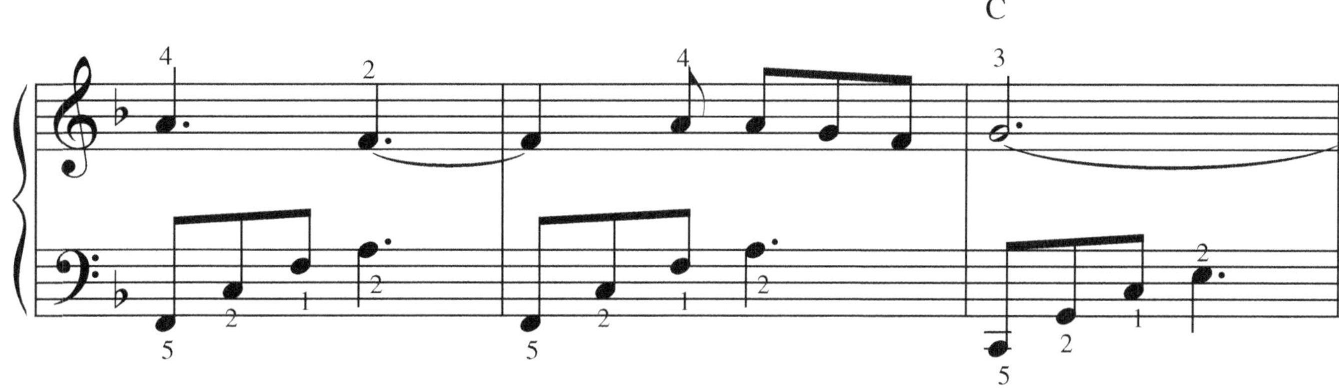

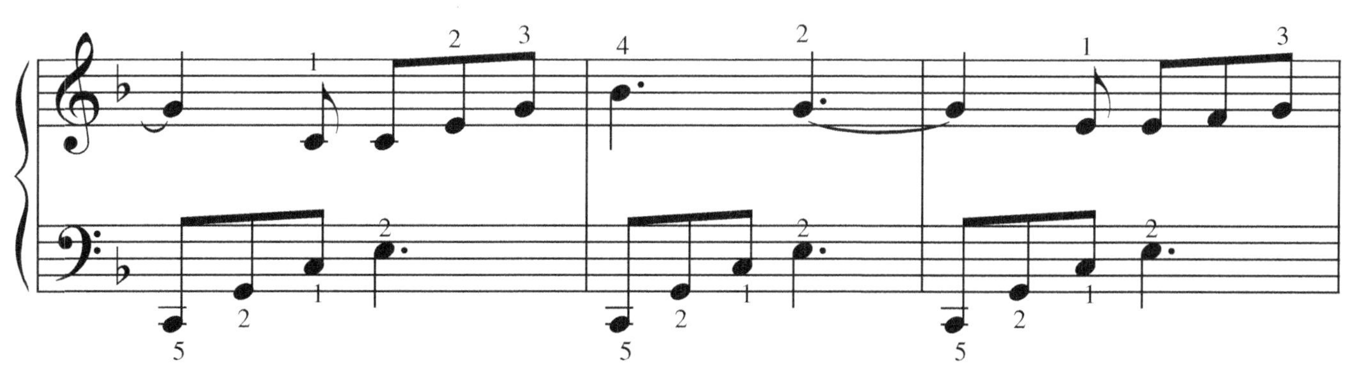

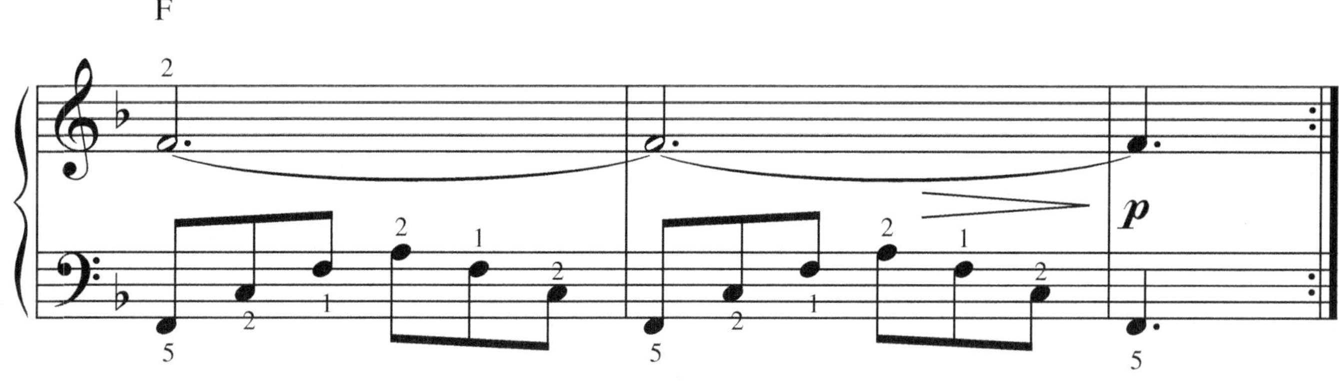

On Top of Old Smokey

United States (1925)

Unknown composer
Roud 414
Arr. Bobby Cyr

♩. = 54

F

mf

C G

C

F C

On Top of Old Smokey

Arpeggios with thirds played on black keys

Exercise: Play the following arpeggios with the left hand.

Sailing, Sailing Over The Bounding Main

England (1880)

James Frederick Swift
(1847–1931)
Arr. Bobby Cyr

♩. = 80

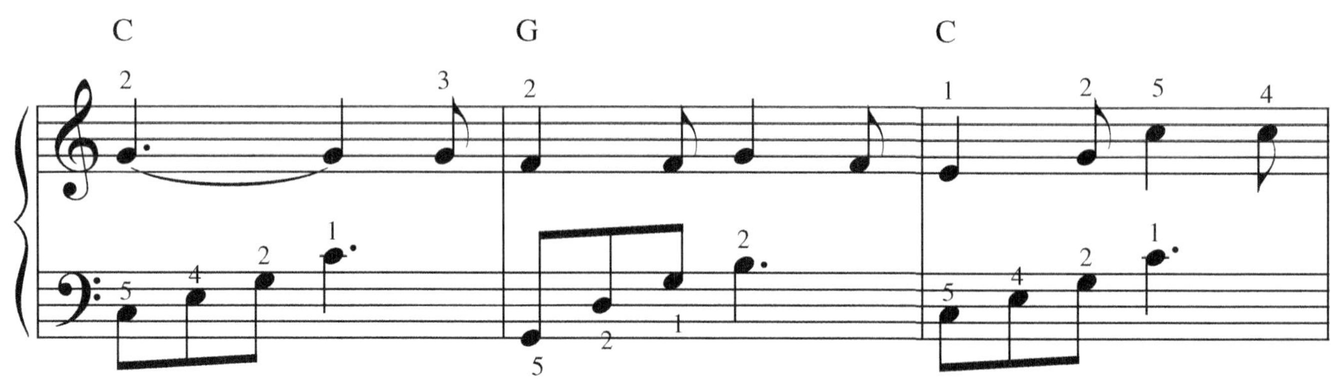

Sailing, Sailing Over The Bounding Main

Bring Back My Bonnie to Me

My Bonnie Lies Over The Ocean
Scotland (1881)

Charles E. Pratt
(1841-1902)
Arr. Bobby Cyr

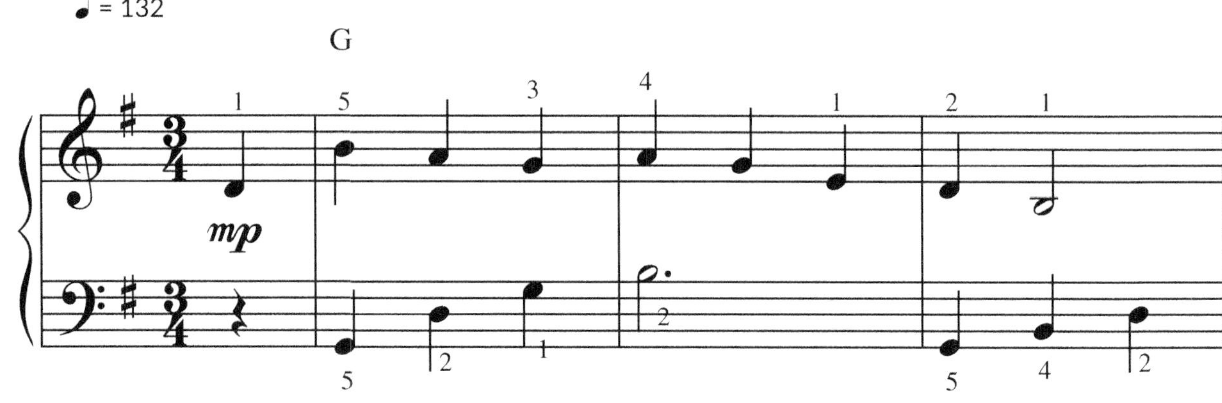

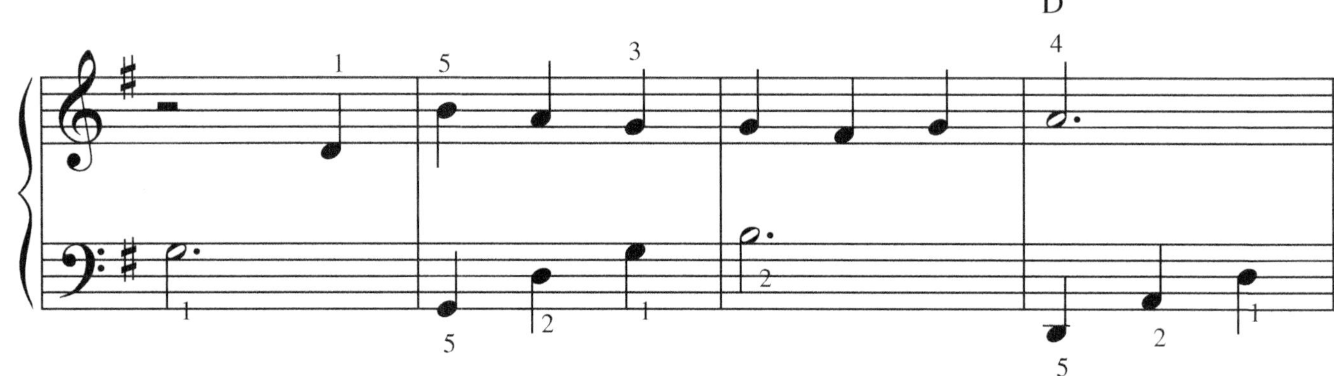

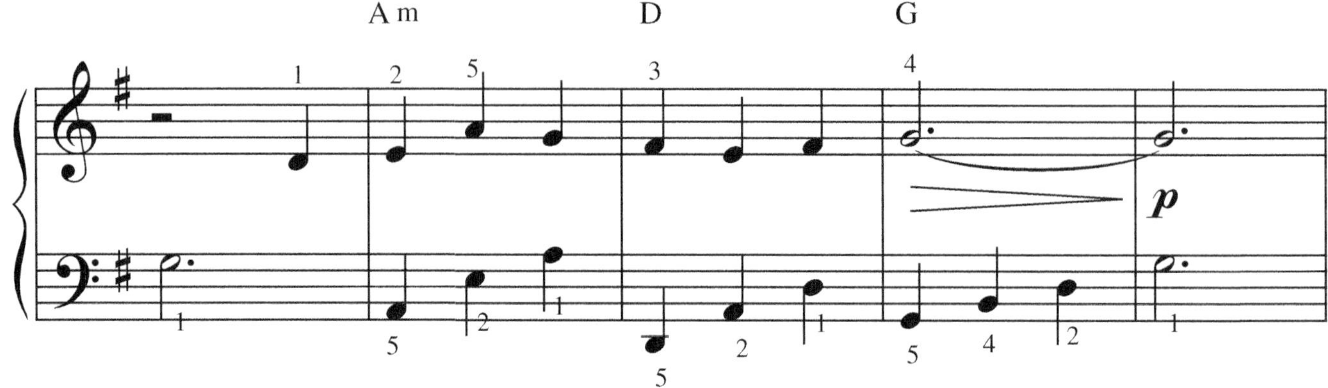

Bring Back My Bonnie to Me

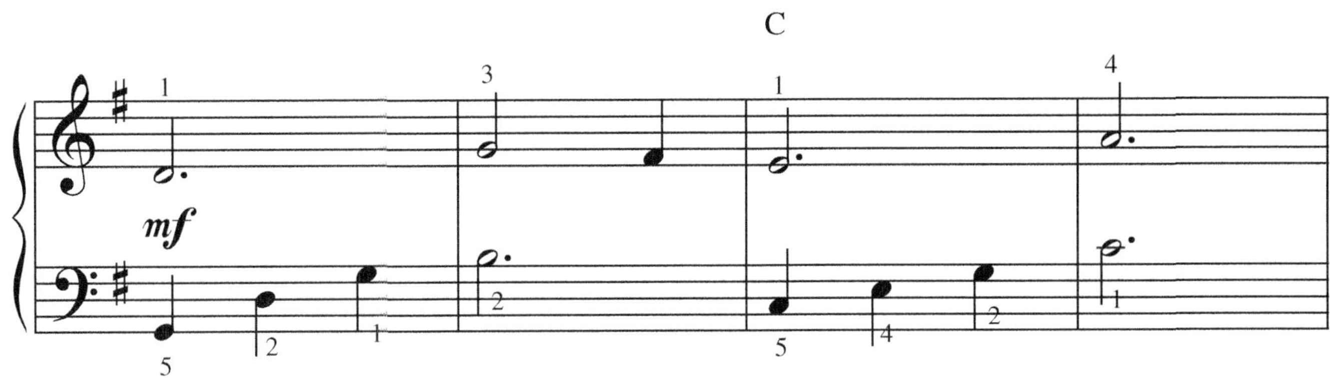

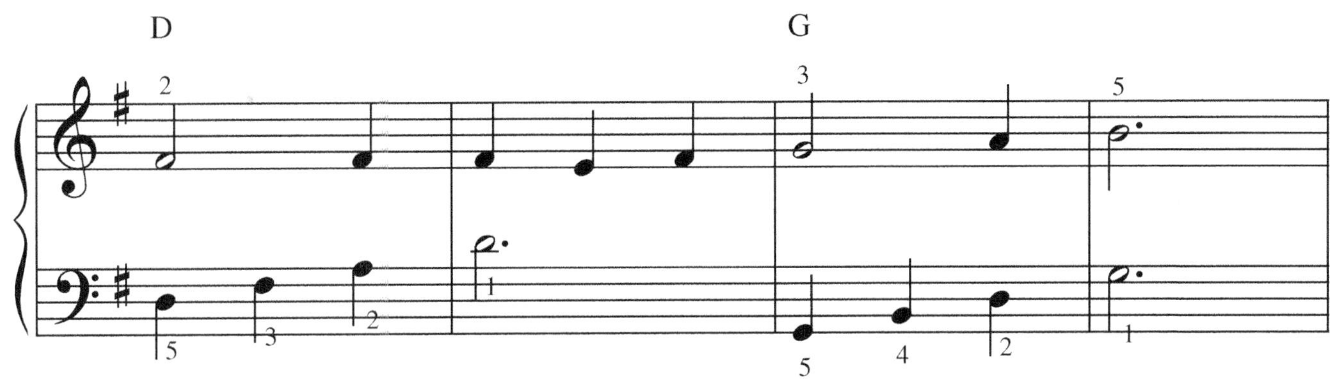

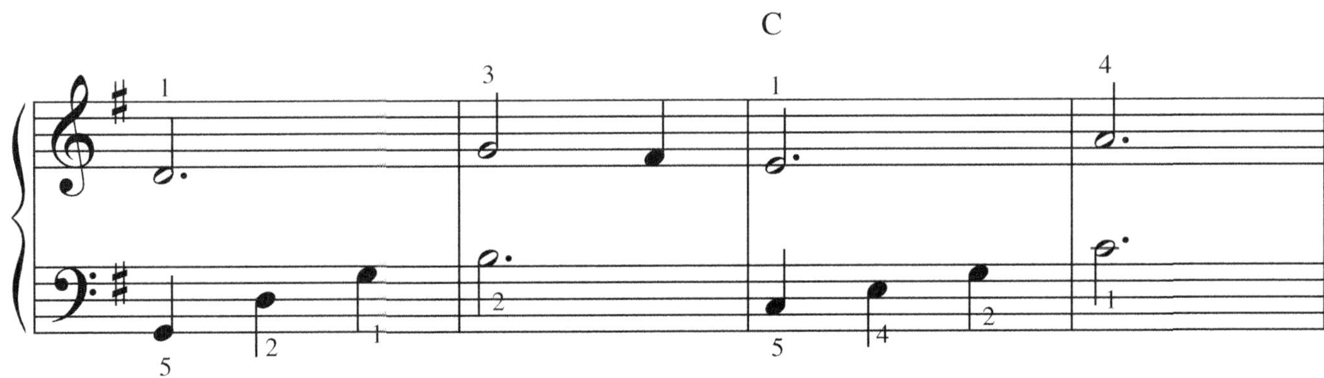

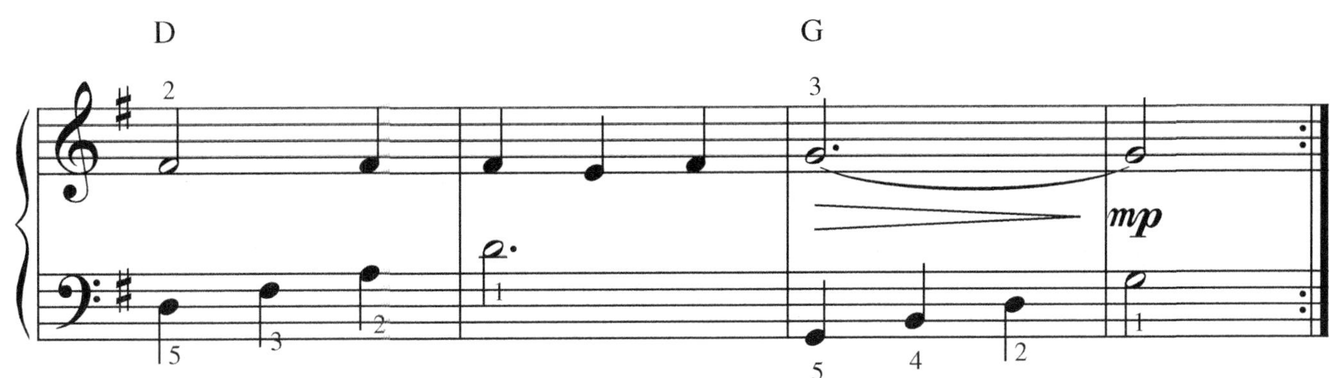

Loch Lomond

Scotland (1841)

Unknown composer
Roud 9598
Arr. Bobby Cyr

♩ = 72

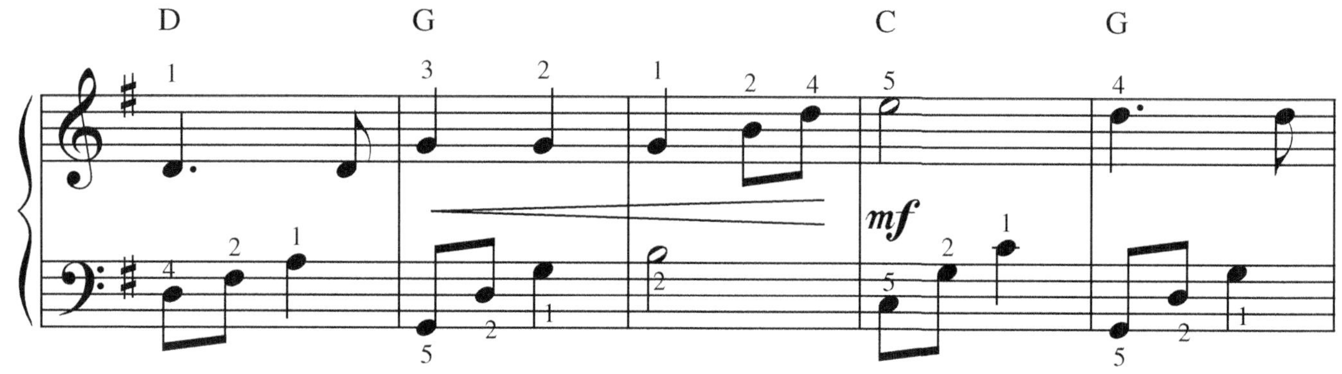

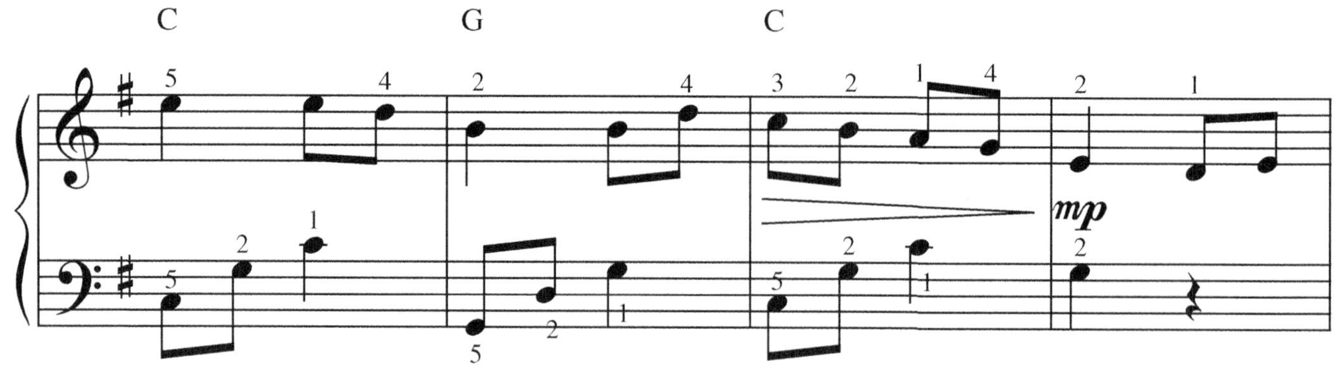

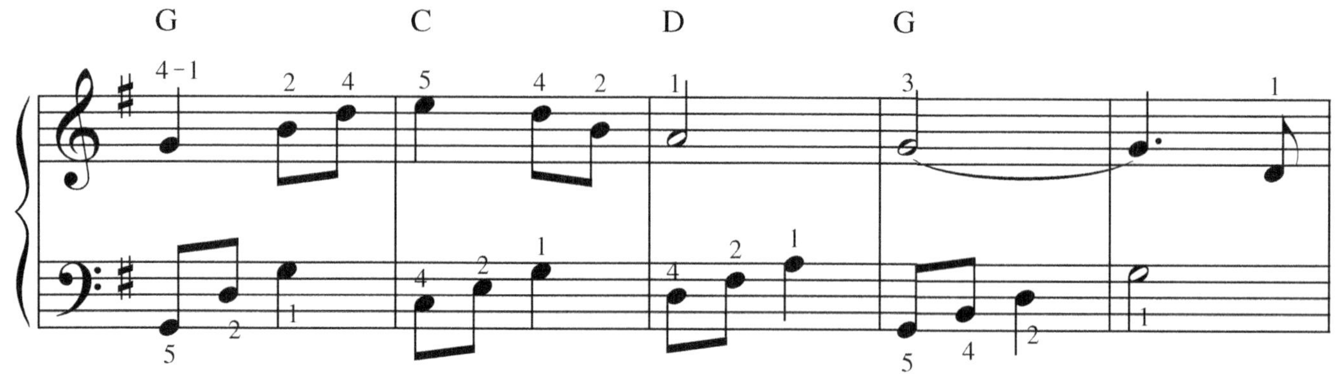

Loch Lomond

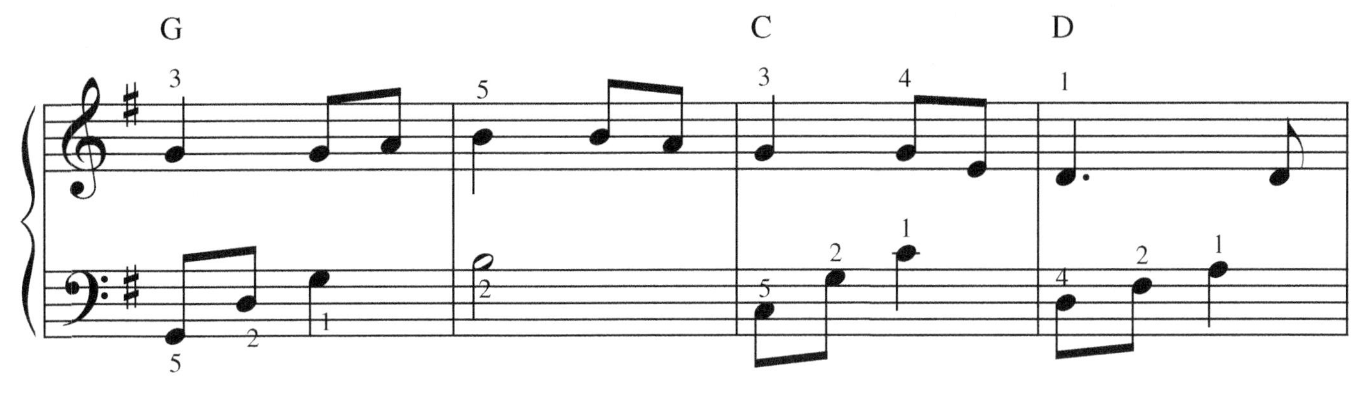

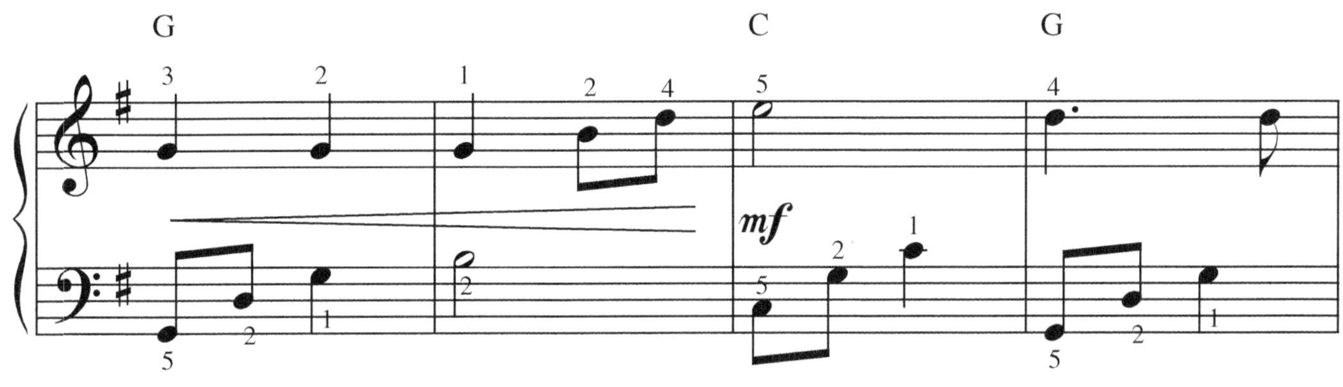

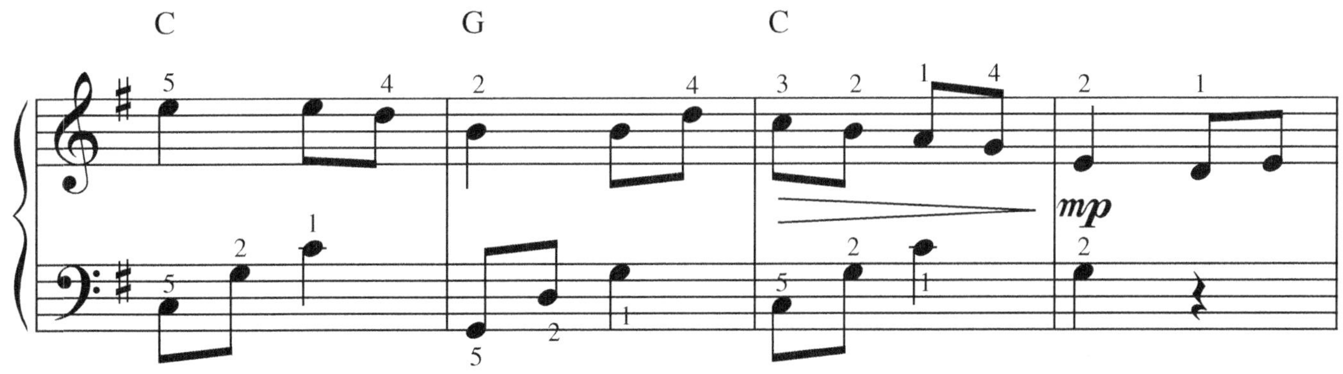

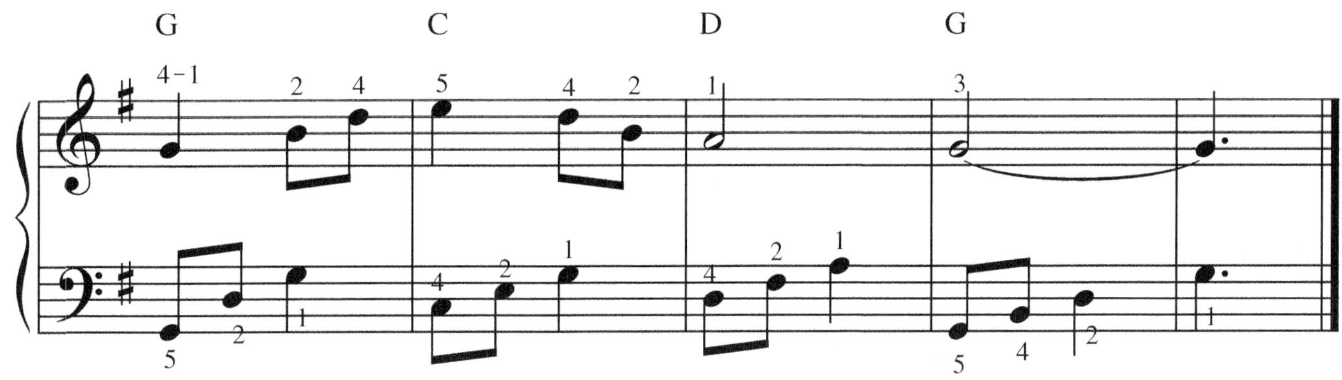

Black Is the Color

United States (1915)

Unknown composer
Roud 3103
Arr. Bobby Cyr

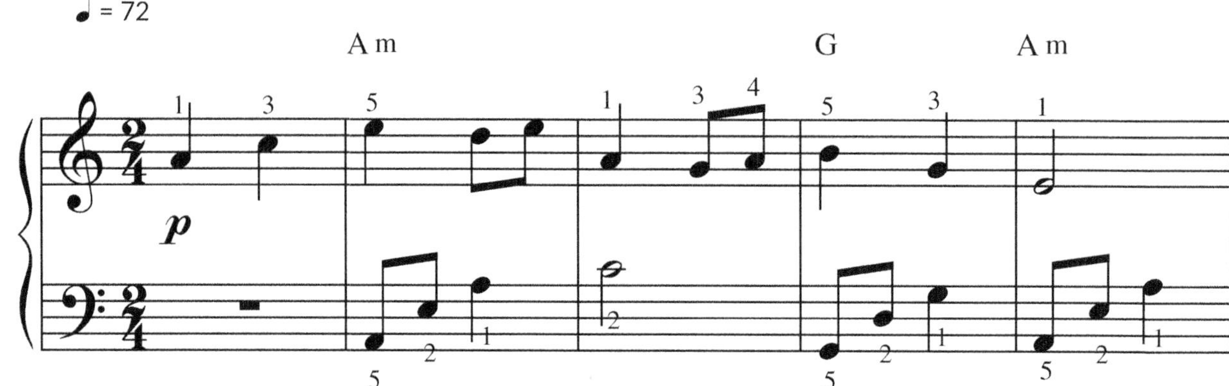

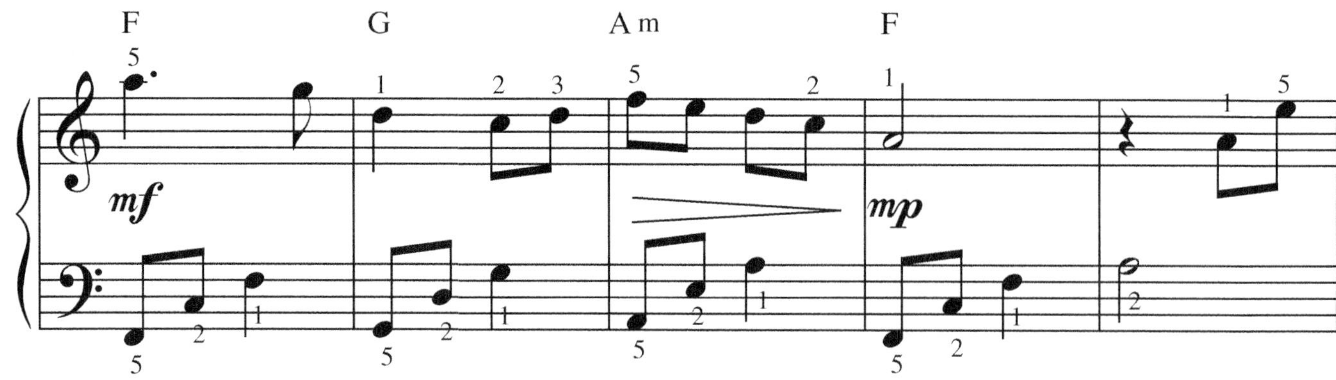

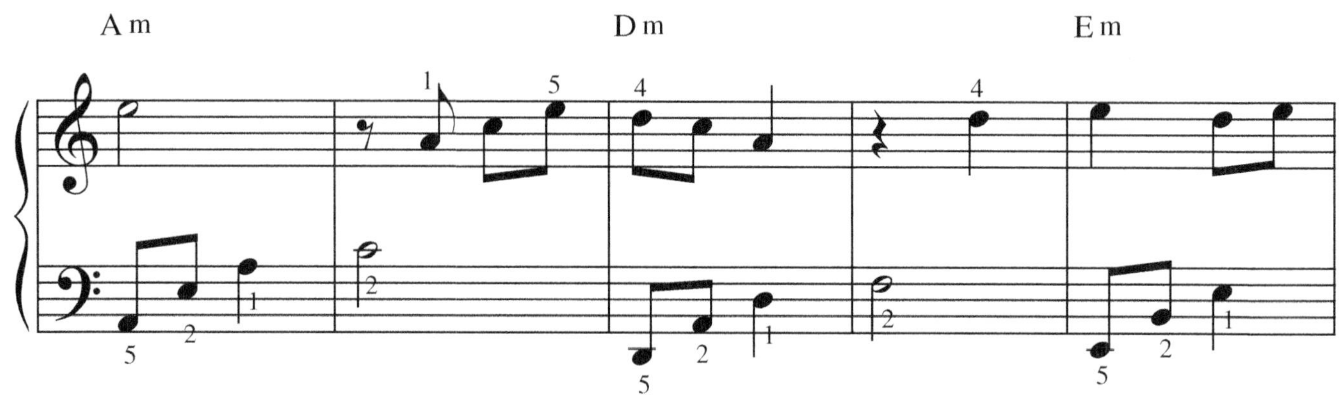

Black Is the Color

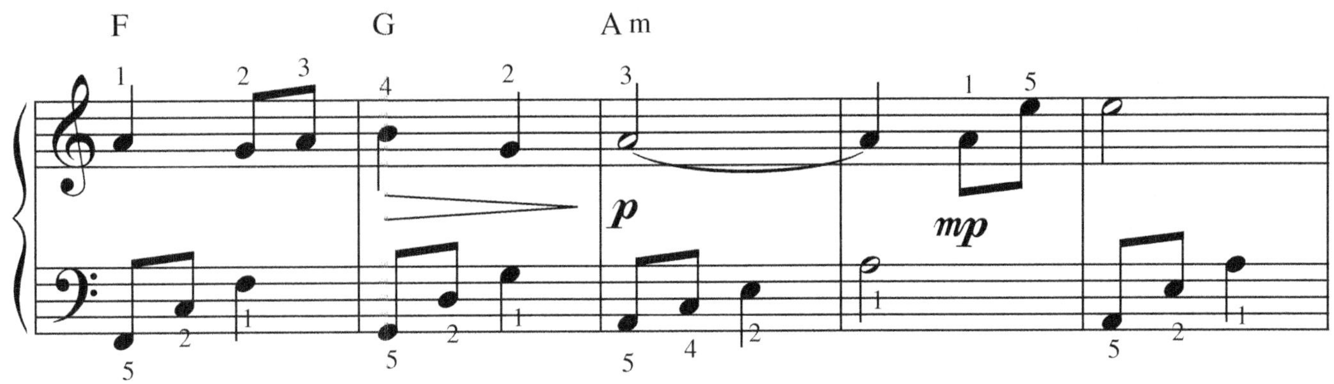

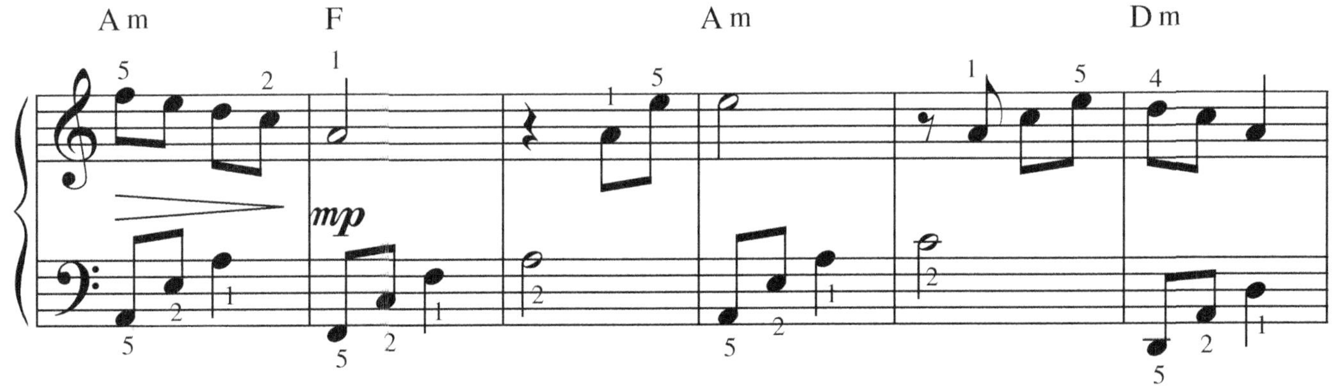

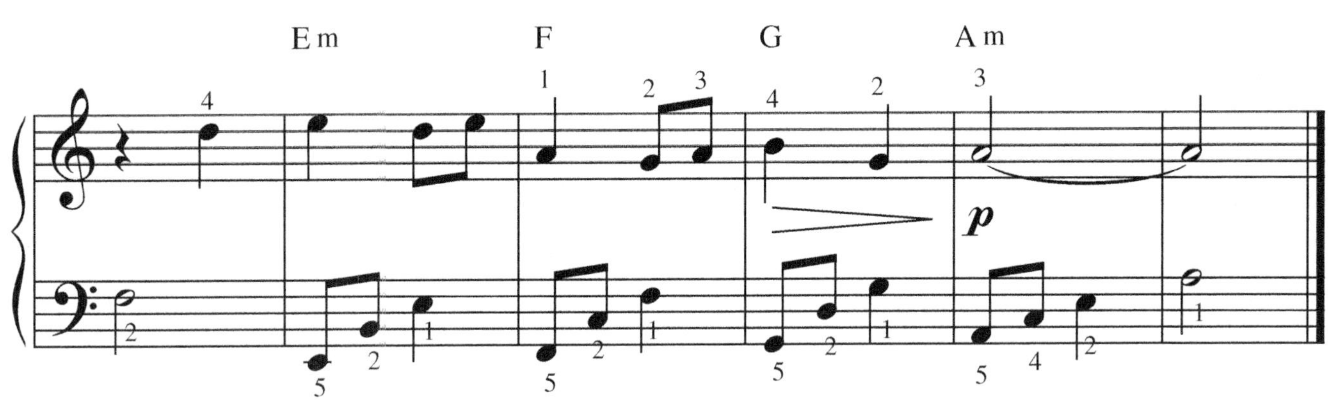

Level 12 pieces

Seventh chords are made up of four notes.
Sometimes the third or fifth is omitted from a seventh chord.

G7 chord (G7)

Santa Lucia

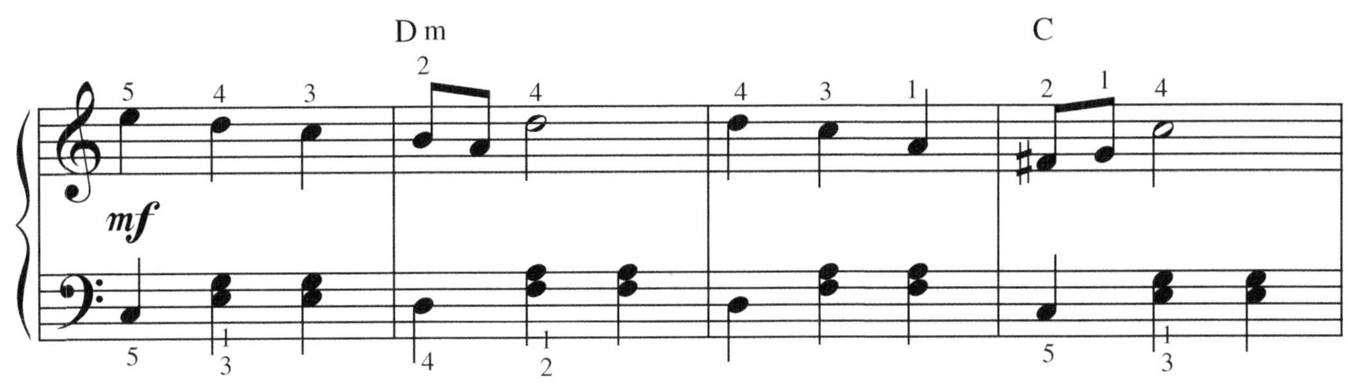

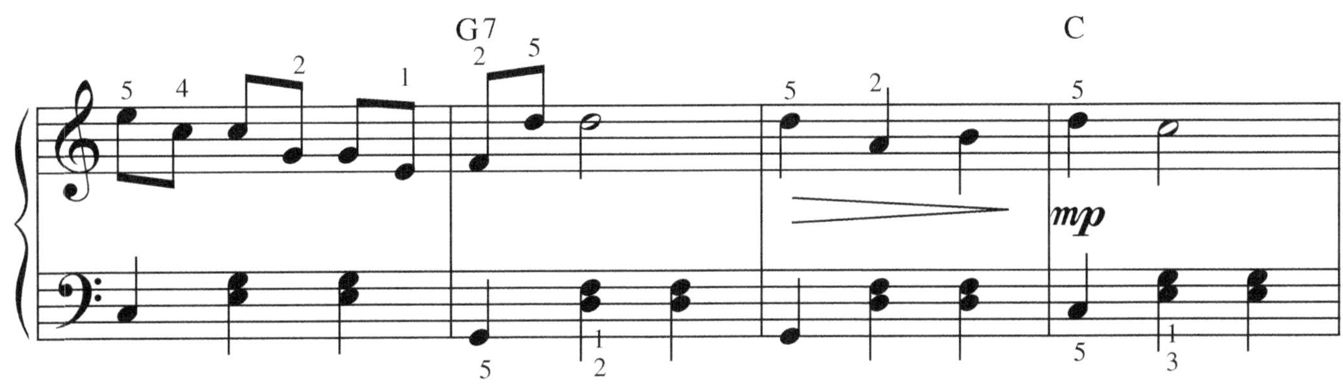

Brahms's Lullaby

Wiegenlied
Austria (1868)

Johannes Brahms
(1833-1897)
Arr. Bobby Cyr

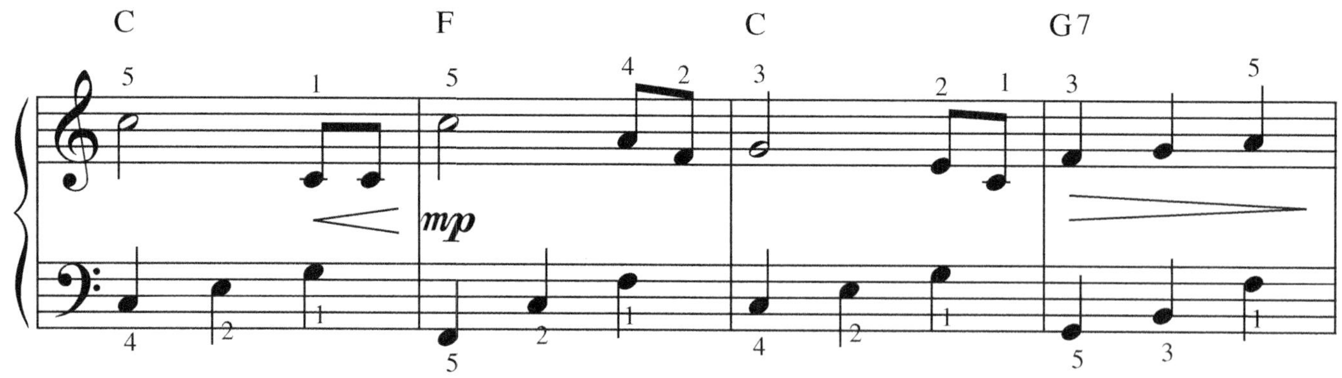

The Yellow Rose of Texas

United States (1859)

J.K.
Arr. Bobby Cyr

Vienna Blood Waltz

Wiener Blut
Austria (1873)

Johann Strauss II
(1825-1899)
Arr. Bobby Cyr

♩ = 144

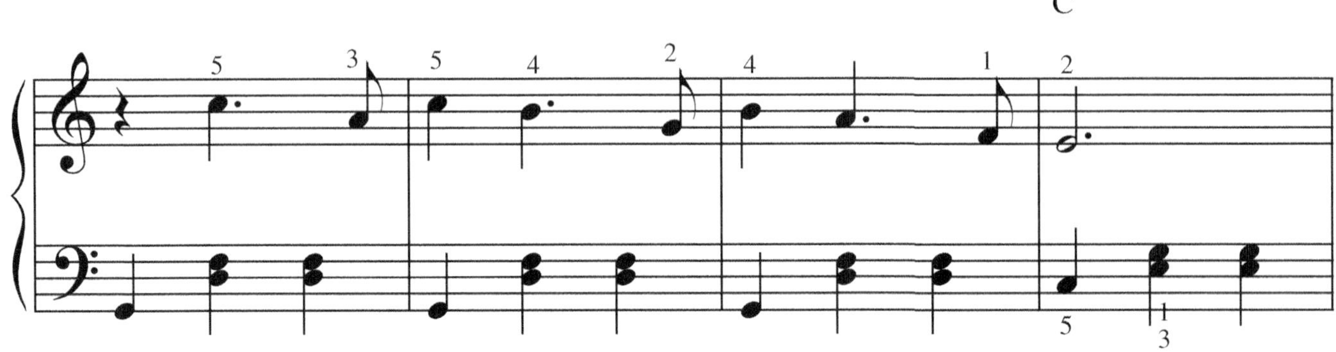

Vienna Blood Waltz

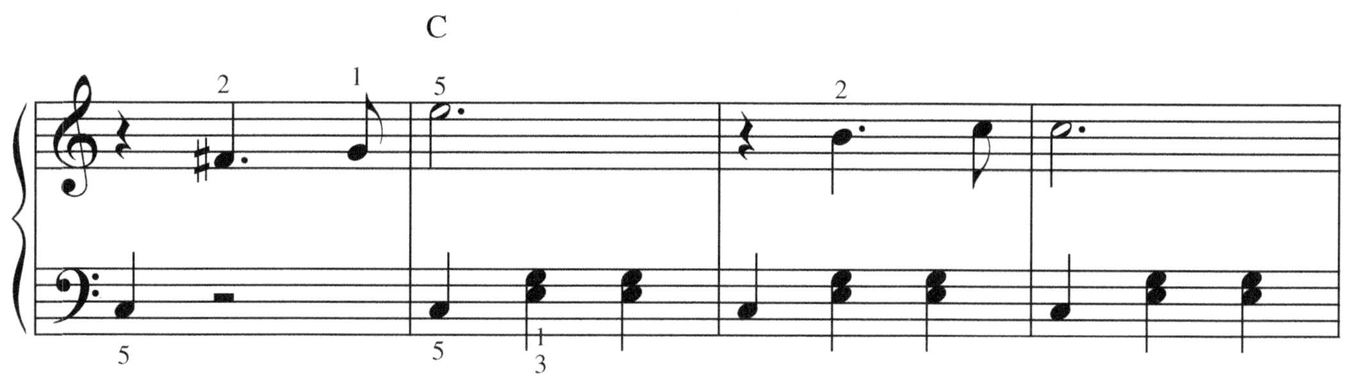

Sweet Evelina

United States (1863)

Thomas Brigham Bishop
(1835-1905)
Arr. Bobby Cyr

Sweet Evelina

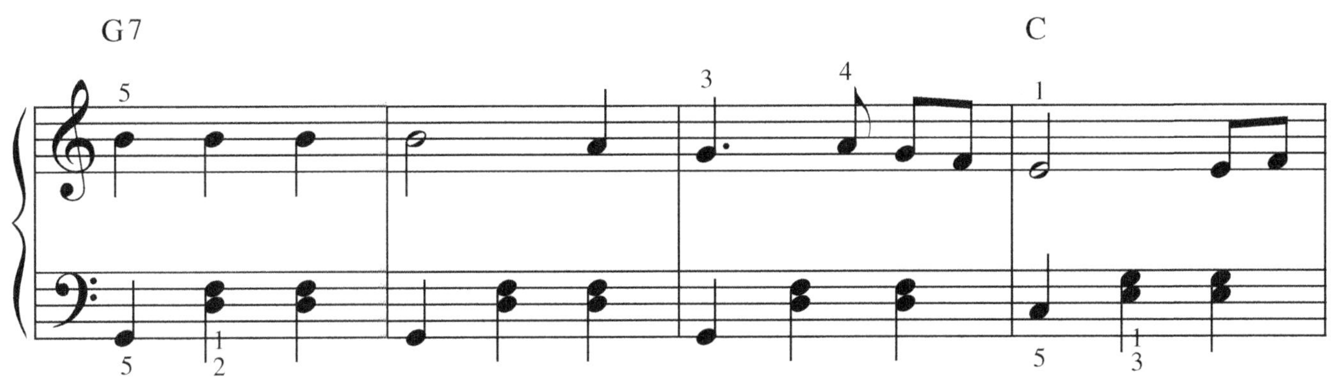

Oh My Darling, Clementine

United States (1884)

Unknown composer
Roud 9611
Arr. Bobby Cyr

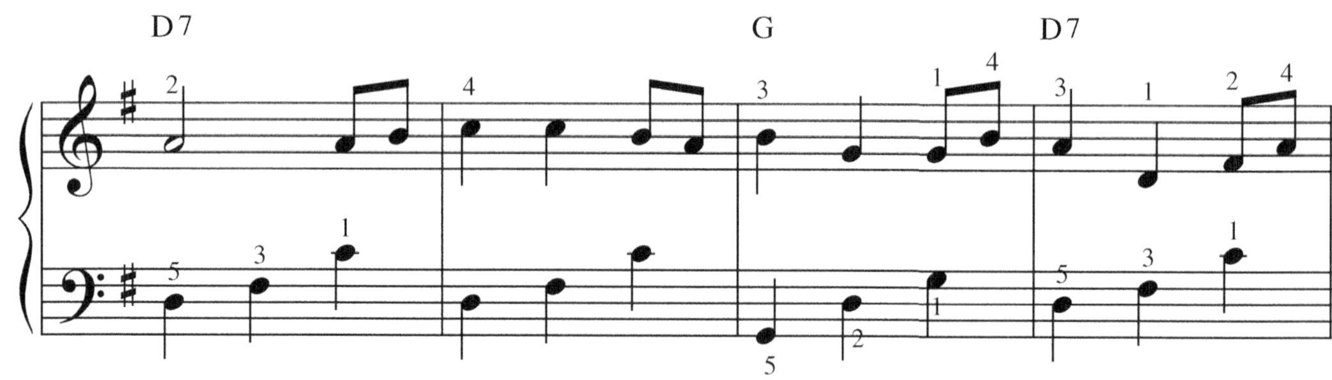

Oh My Darling, Clementine

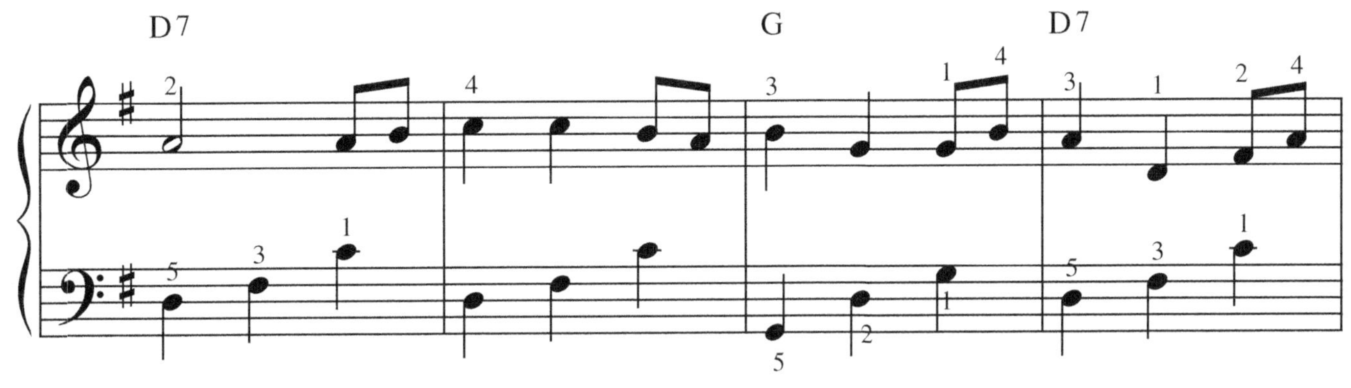

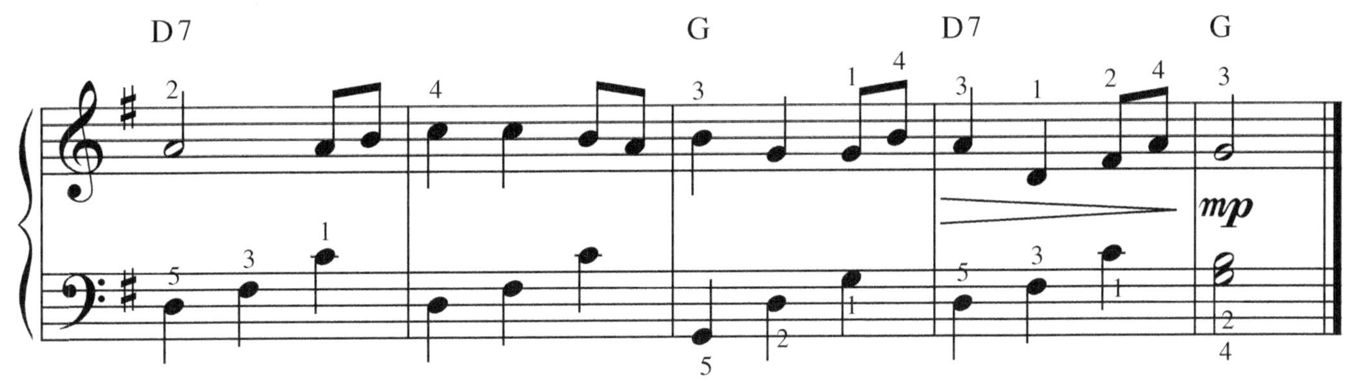

Aloha Oe

Hawaii (1877)

Queen Liliuokalani
(1838-1917)
Arr. Bobby Cyr

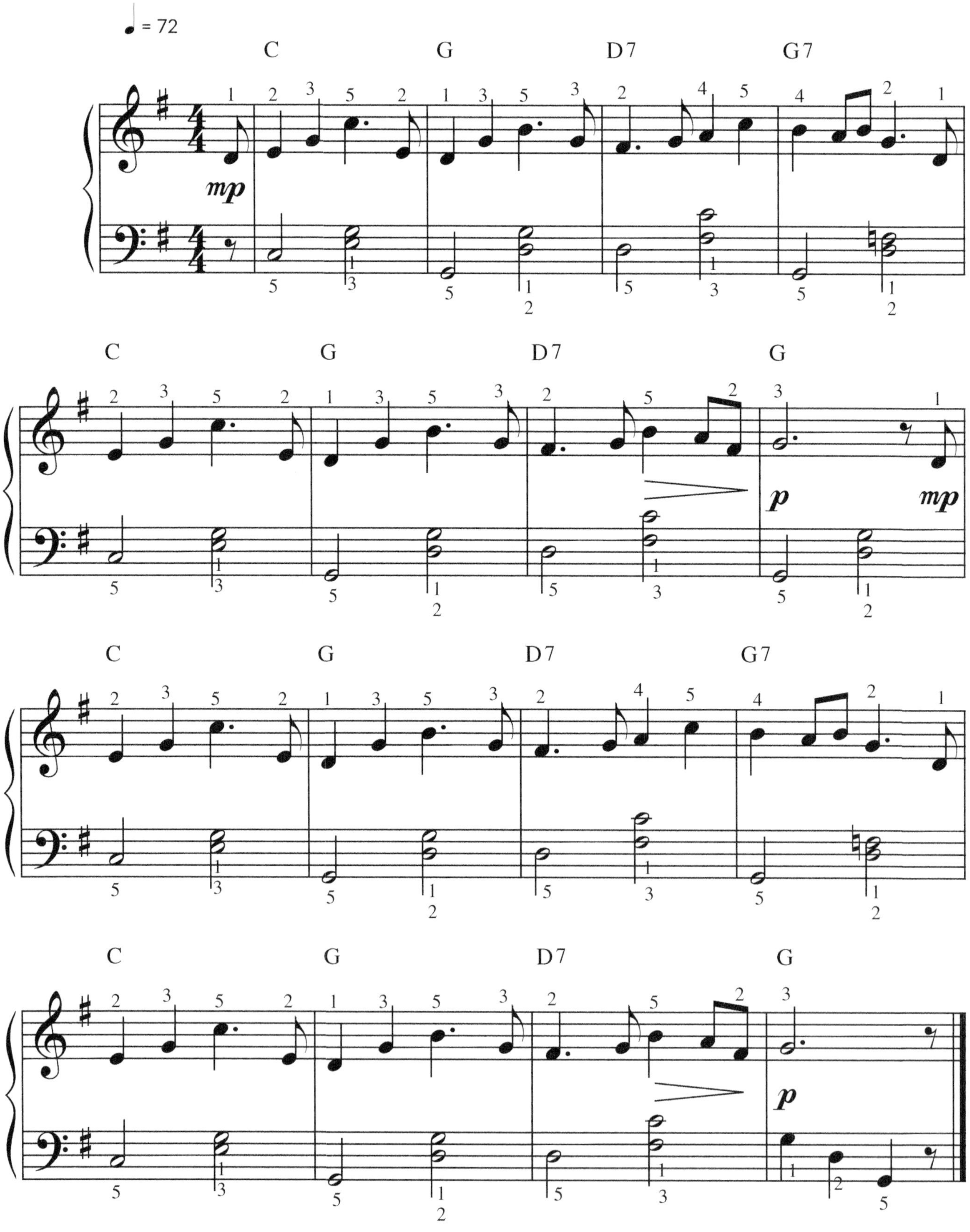

♩ = 72

C G D7 G7

mp

C G D7 G

p *mp*

C G D7 G7

C G D7 G

p

The Wild Colonial Boy

Ireland (1926)

Unknown composer
Roud 677
Arr. Bobby Cyr

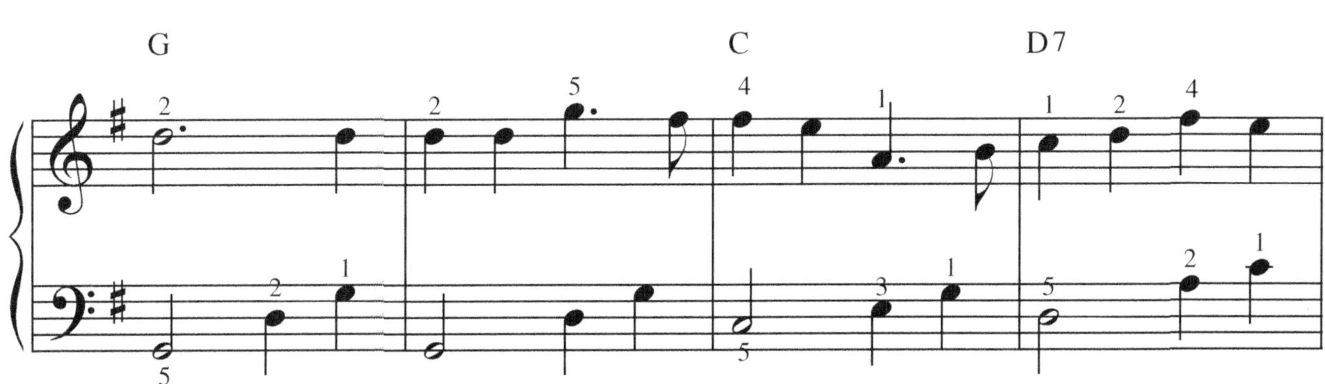

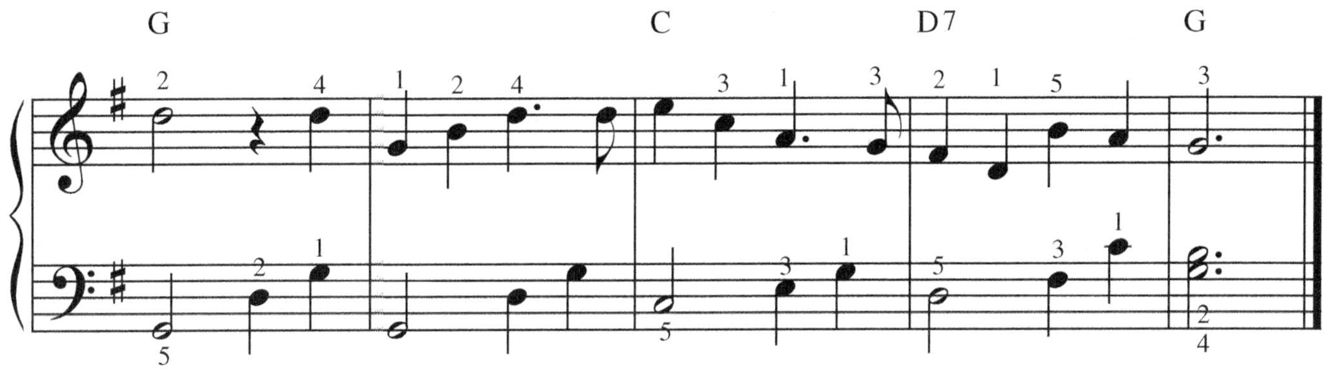

My Wild Irish Rose

United States (1899)

Chauncey Olcott
(1858-1932)
Arr. Bobby Cyr

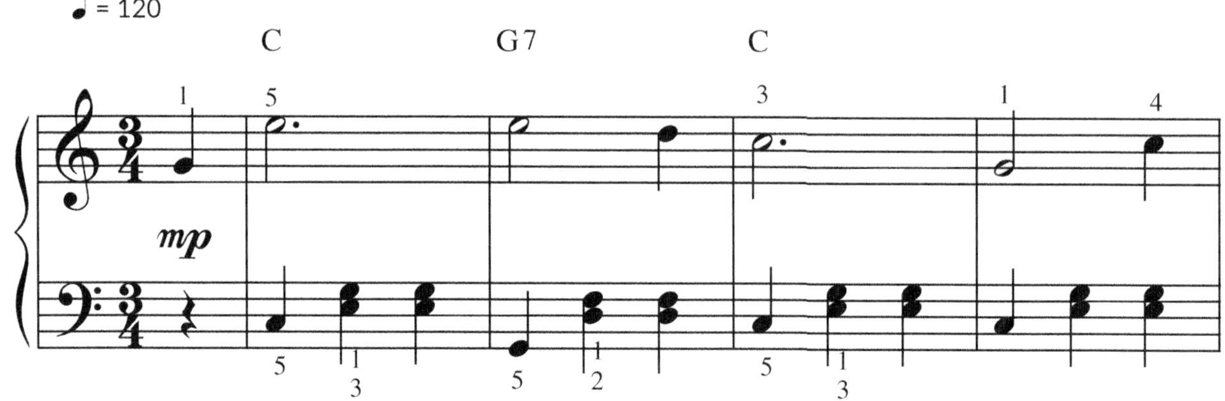

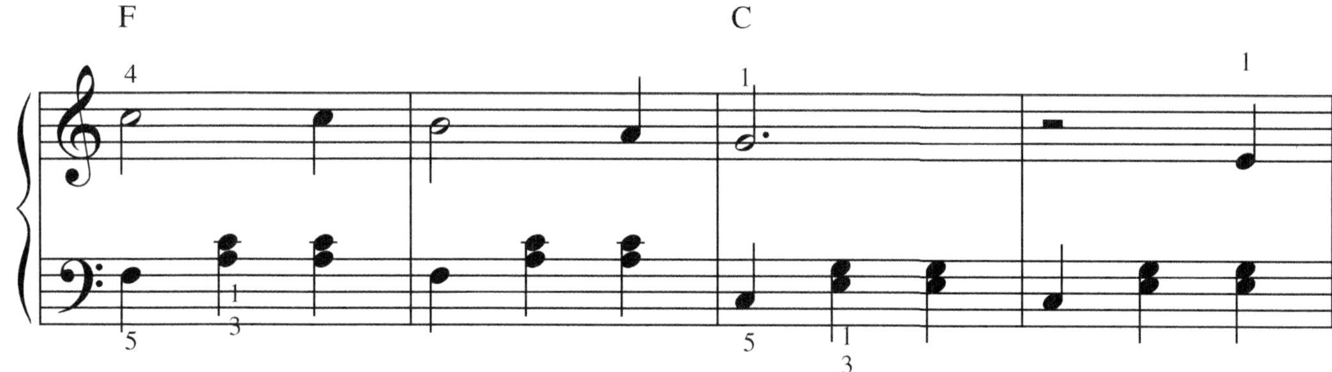

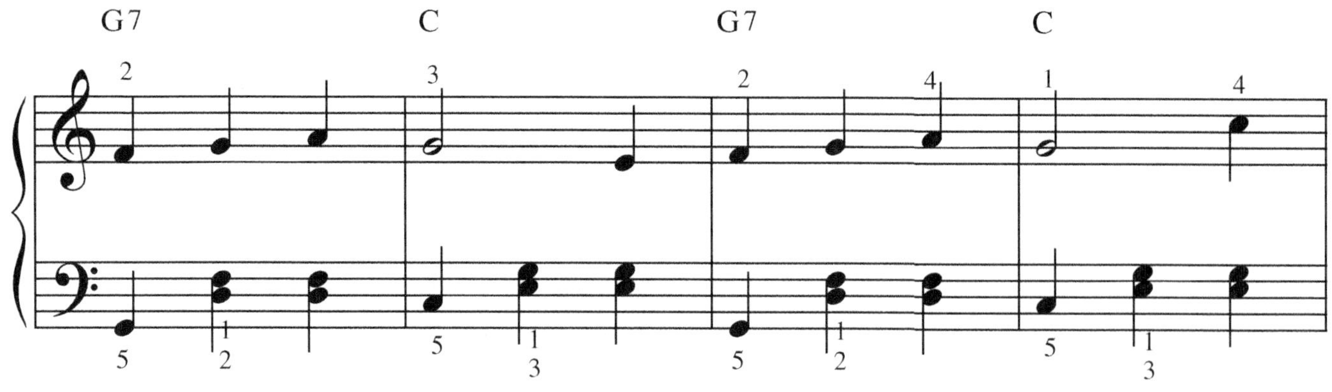

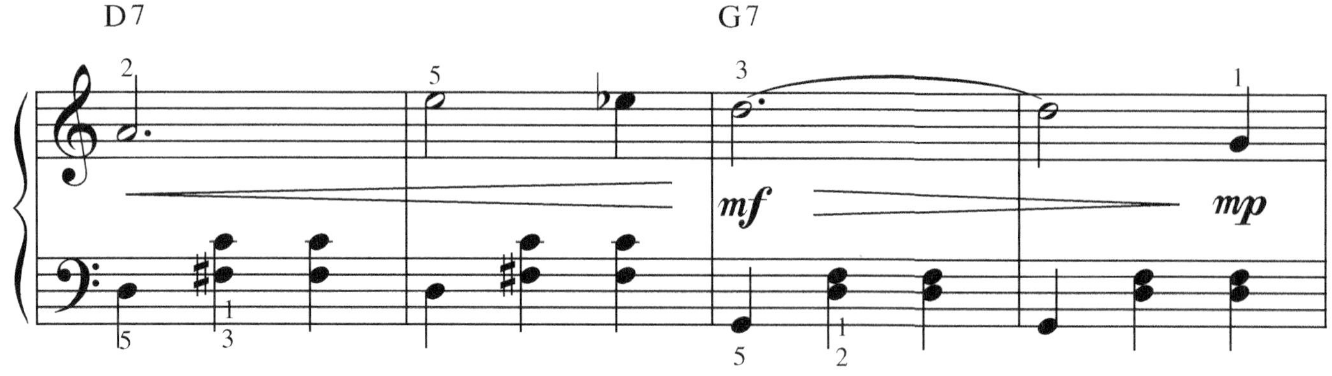

My Wild Irish Rose

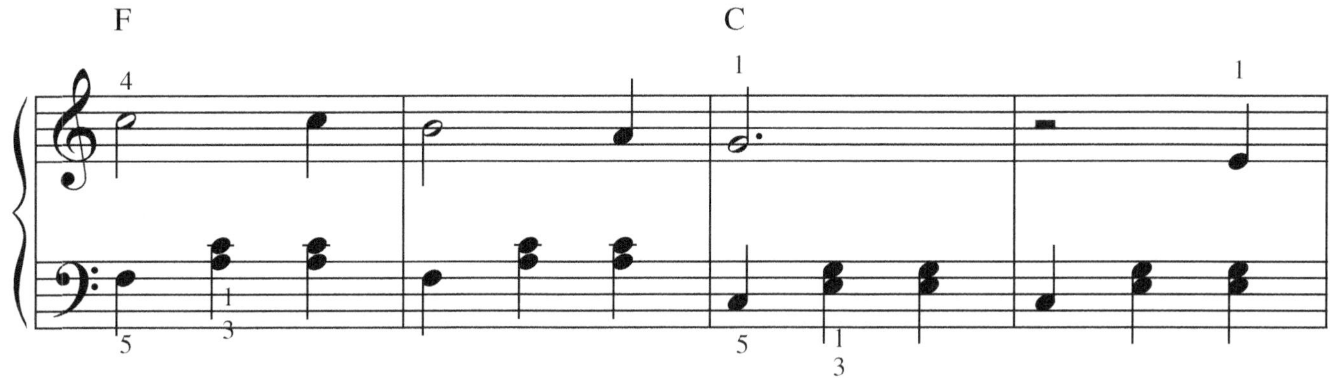

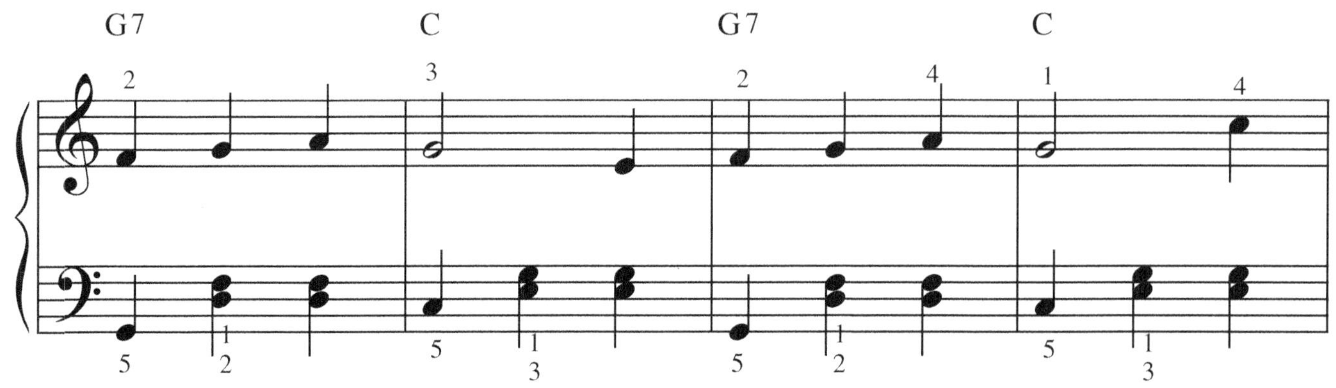

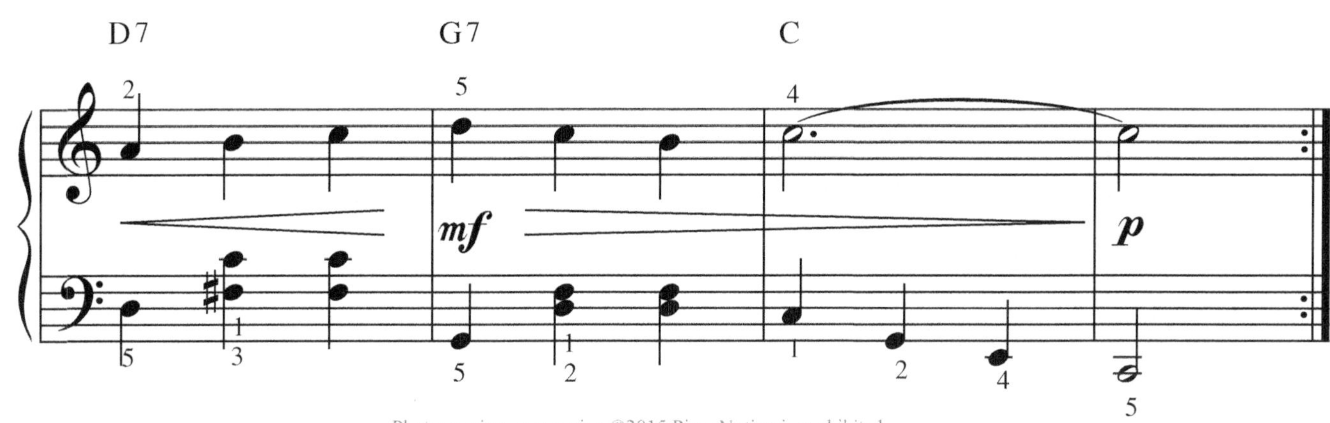

Mexican Hat Dance

Jarabe Tapatío
Mexico

Jesus Gonzalez Rubio
(?-1874)
Arr. Bobby Cyr

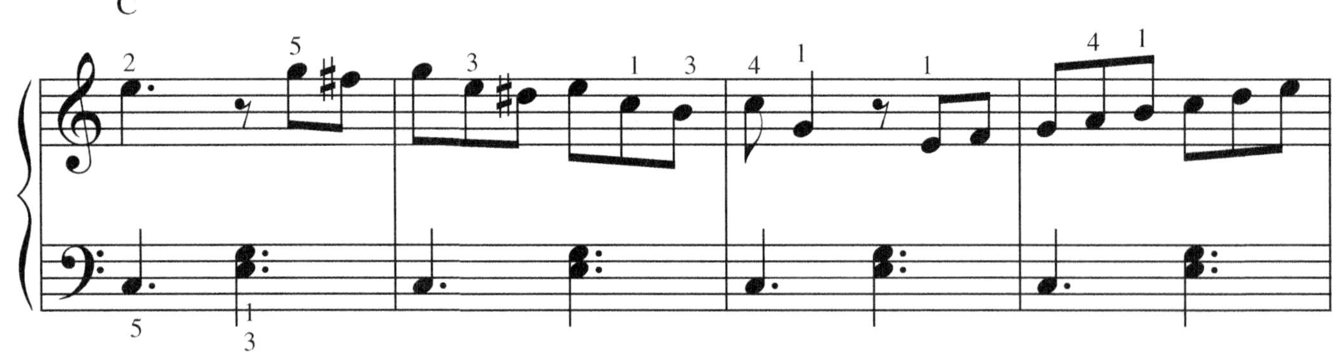

Mexican Hat Dance

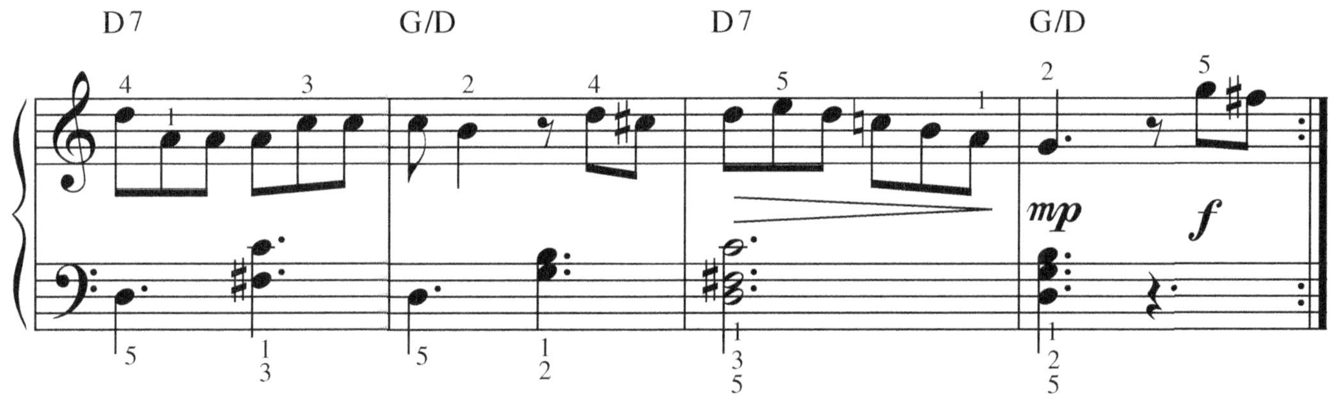

Level 13 pieces

B flat major chord (Bb)

B flat major chord is made up of three notes: B flat, D and F.

Exercise: Play the B flat major chord with the left hand.

Abdul Abulbul Amir

Ireland (1877)

Percy French
(1854–1920)
Arr. Bobby Cyr

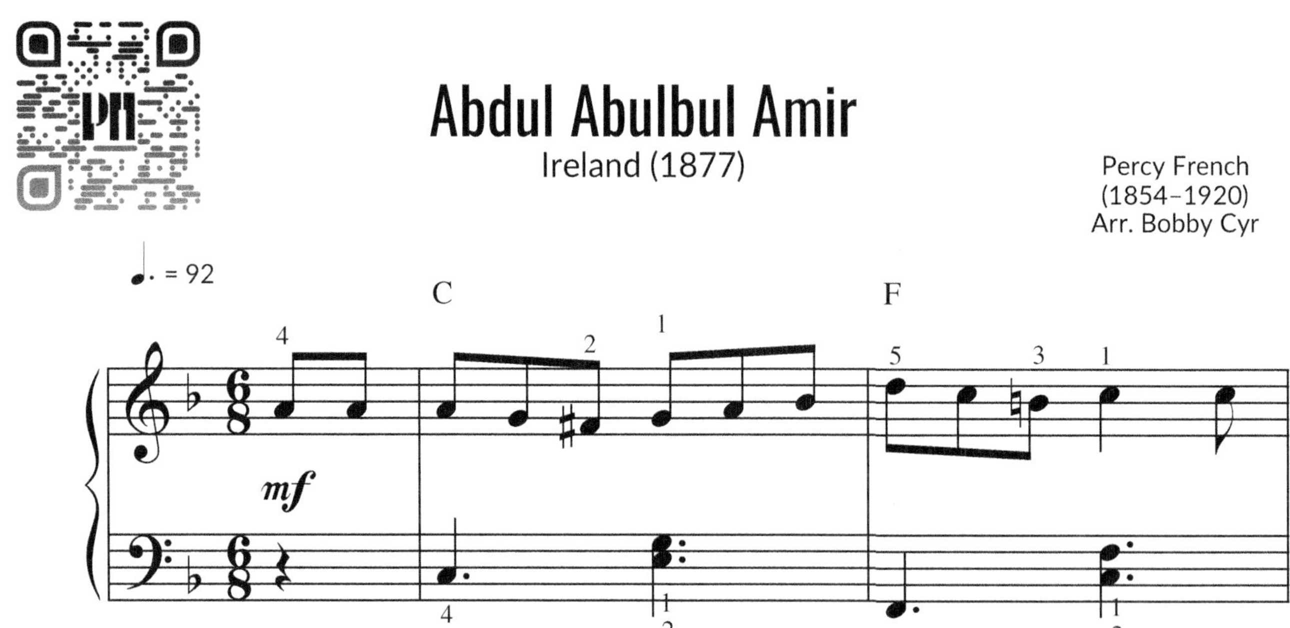

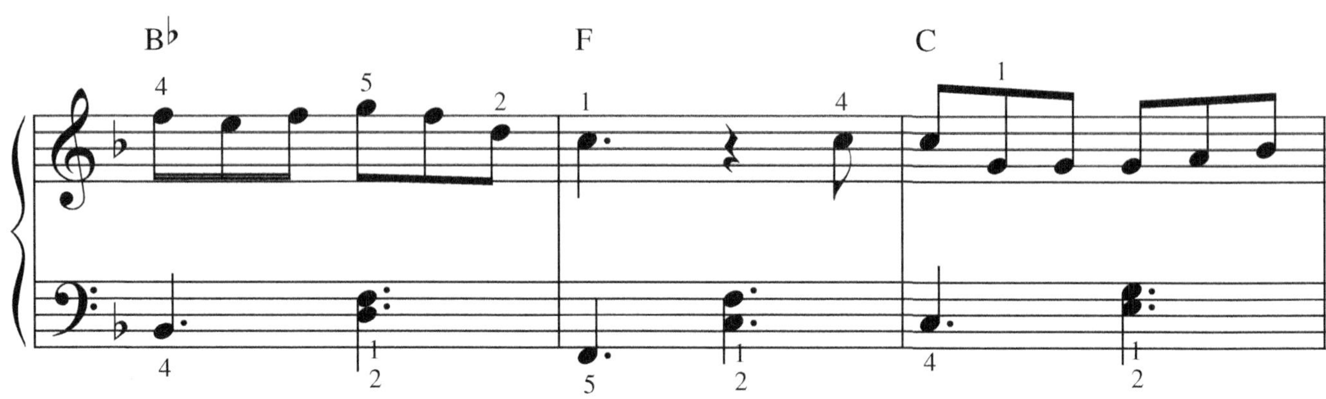

Abdul Abulbul Amir

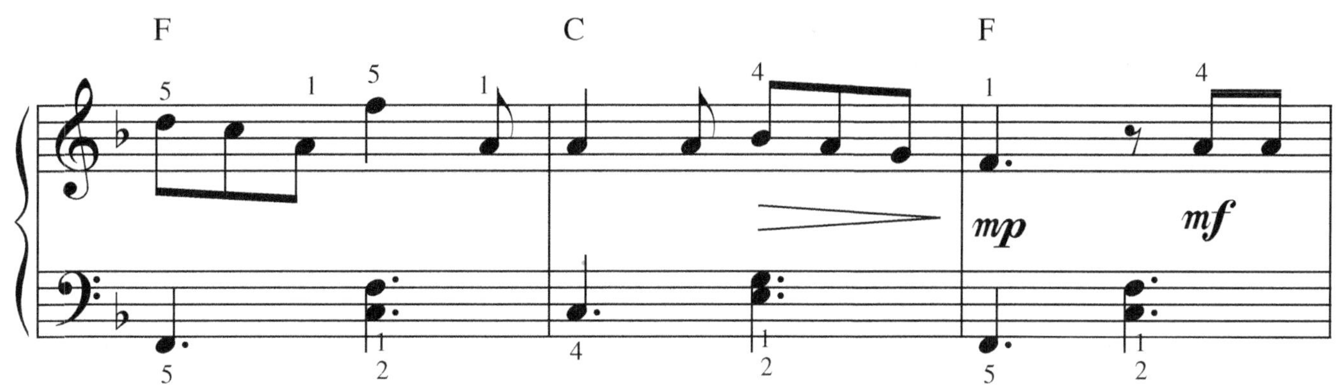

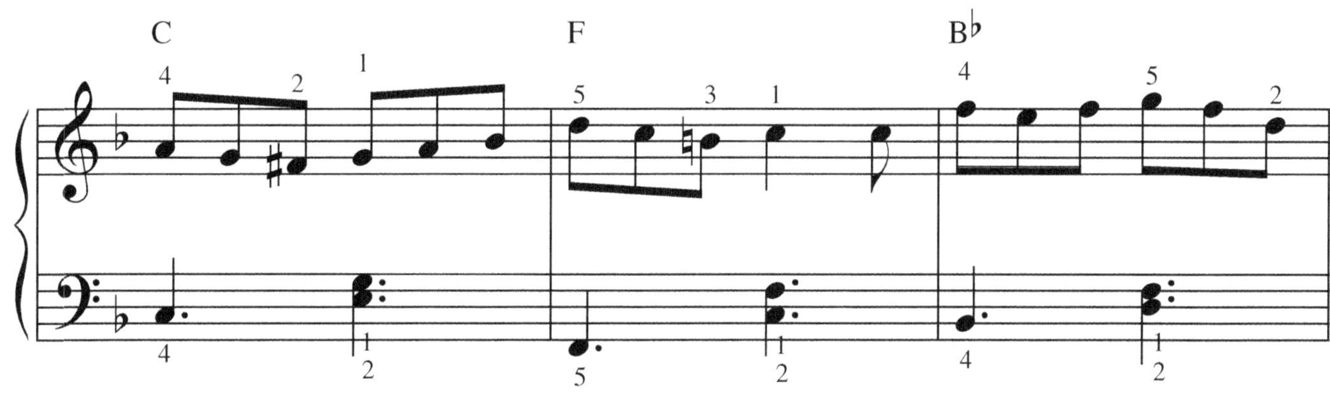

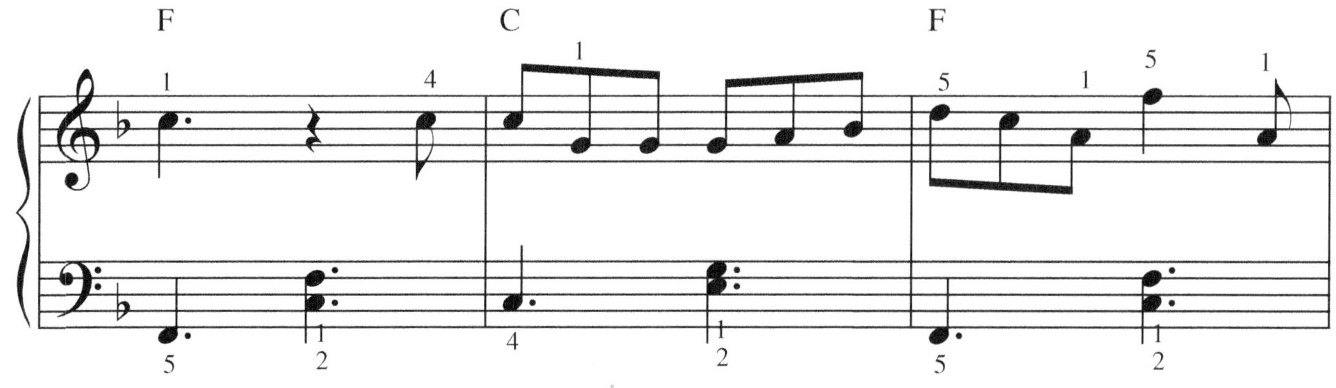

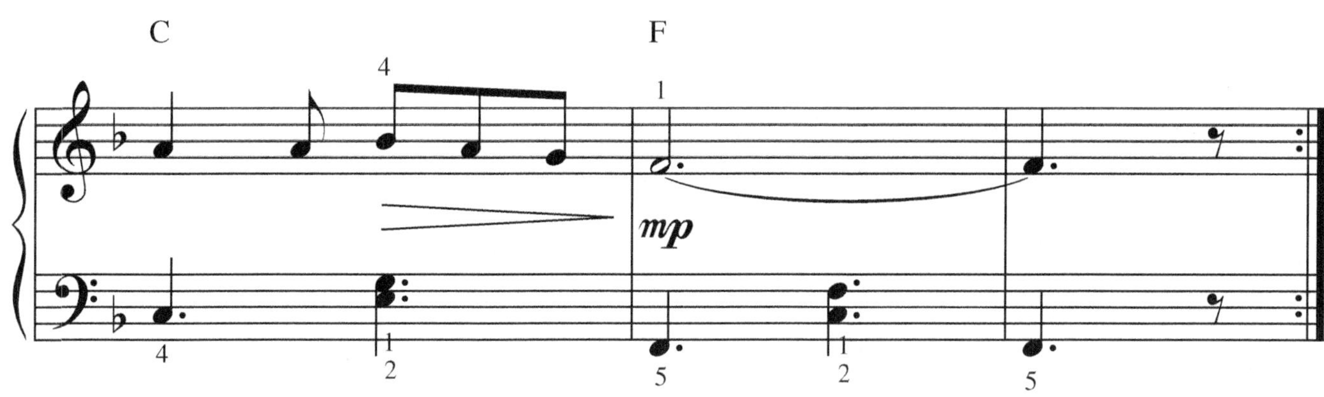

B flat arpeggio (Bb)

It's best to avoid playing the black keys with the 1st and 5th fingers. However, in some cases, this rule doesn't apply.

Exercise: Play the fifth and the octave with the left hand, starting on the 5th finger.

Exercise: Play the B-flat major arpeggio with the left hand.

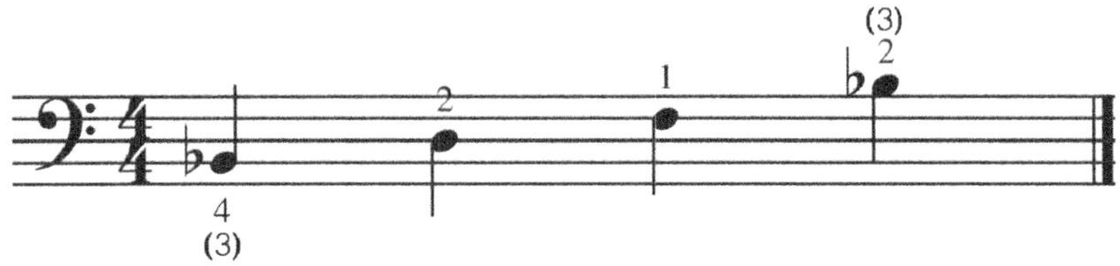

Jasmine Flower

Mo Li Hua
China

Unknown composer
Arr. Bobby Cyr

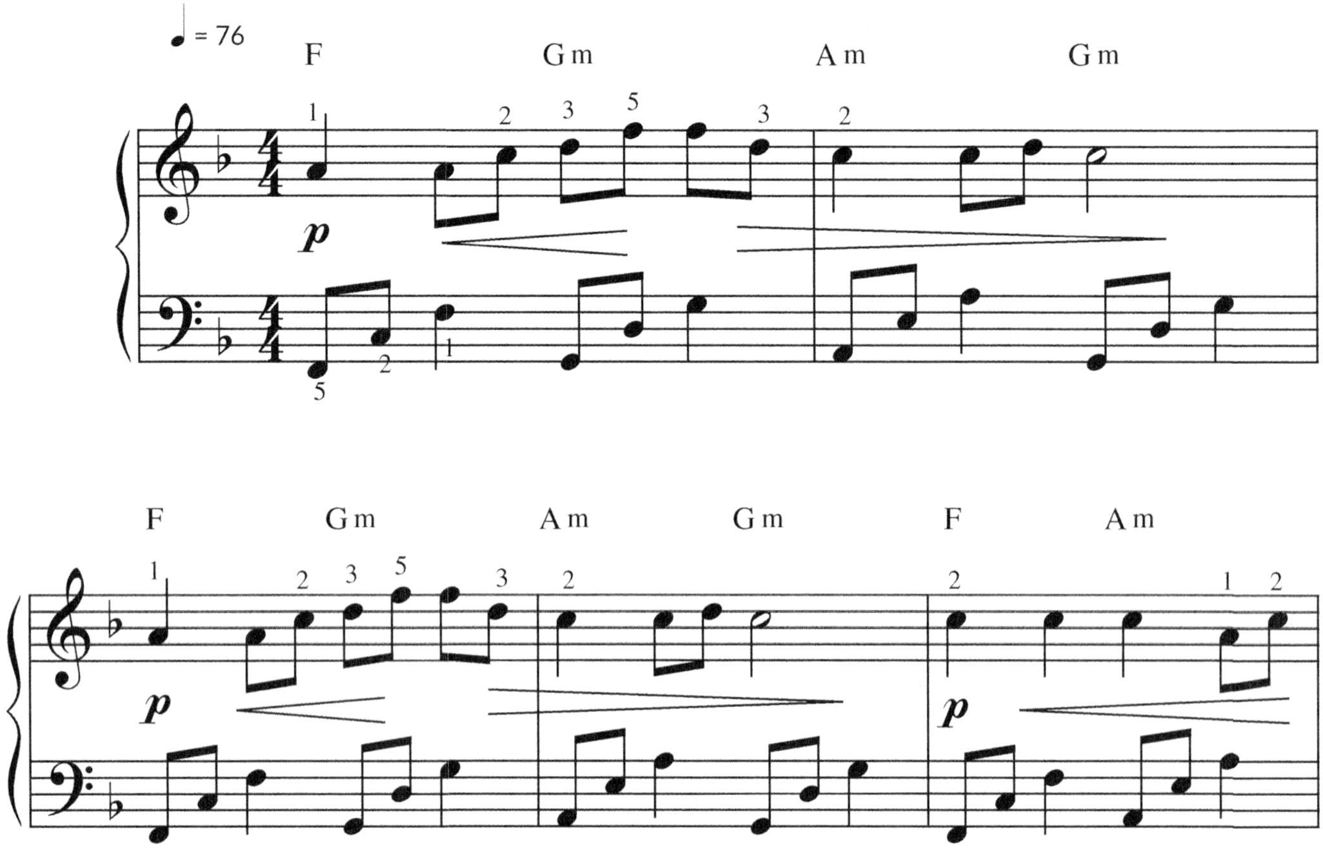

♩ = 76

F Gm Am Gm

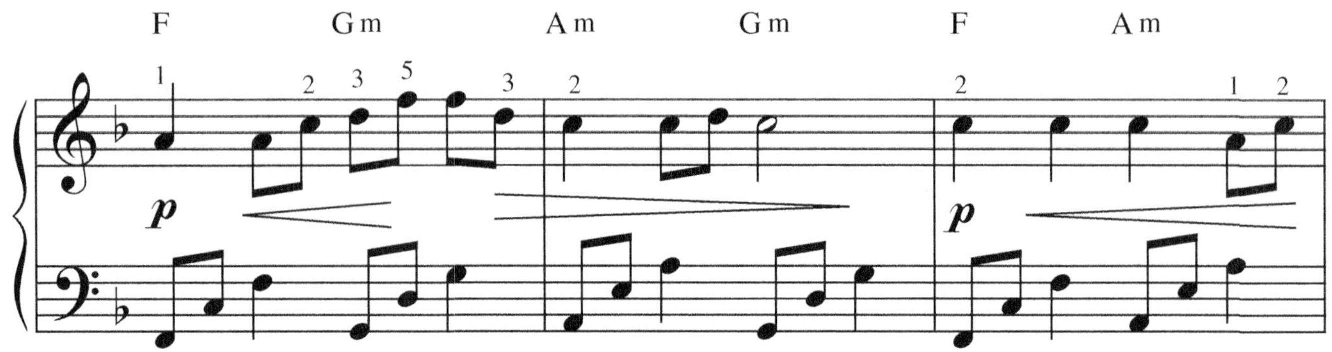

Jasmine Flower

The House of the Rising Sun

Rising Sun Blues
United States

Unknown composer
Roud 6393
Arr. Bobby Cyr

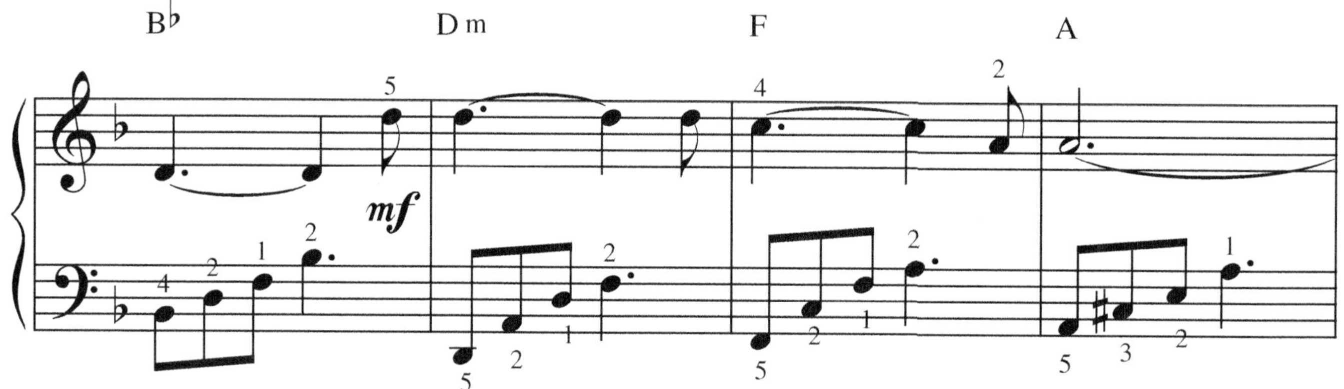

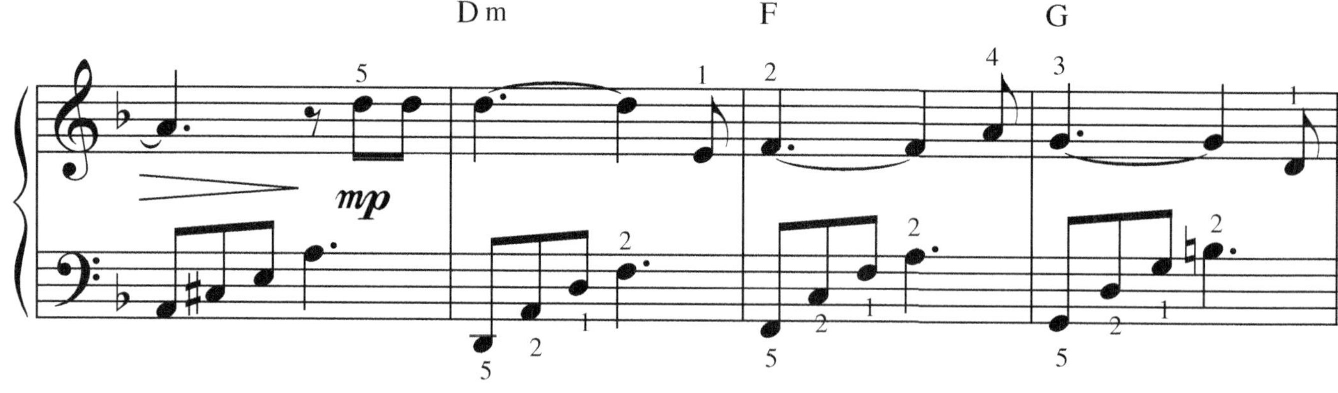

The House of the Rising Sun

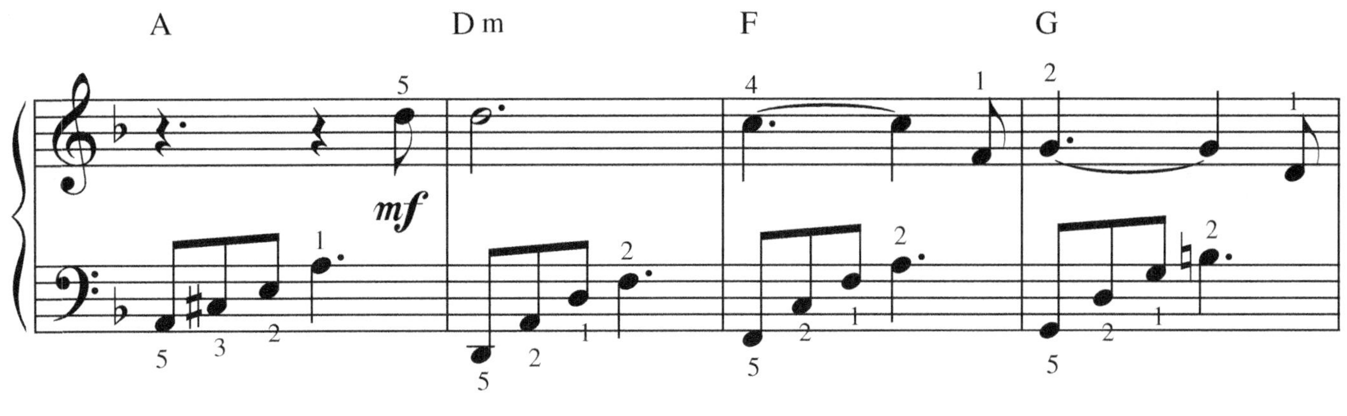

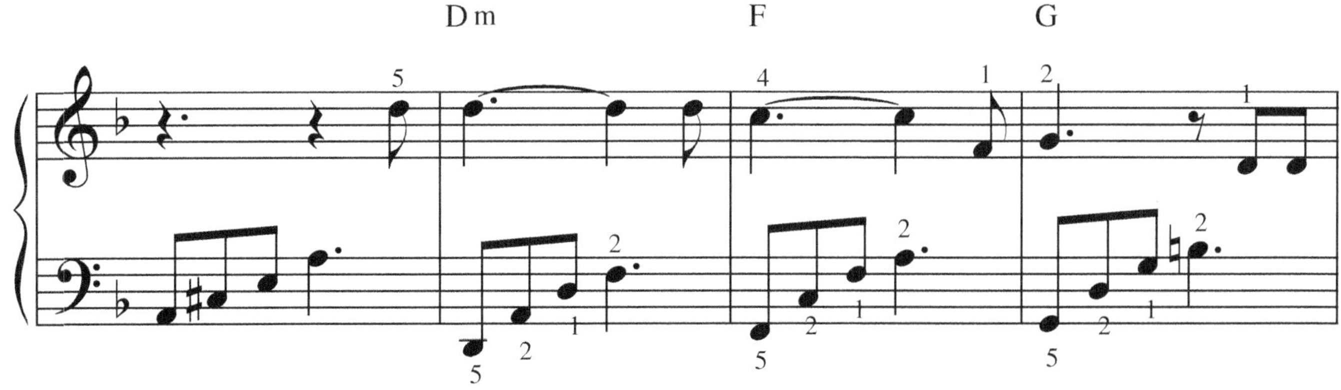

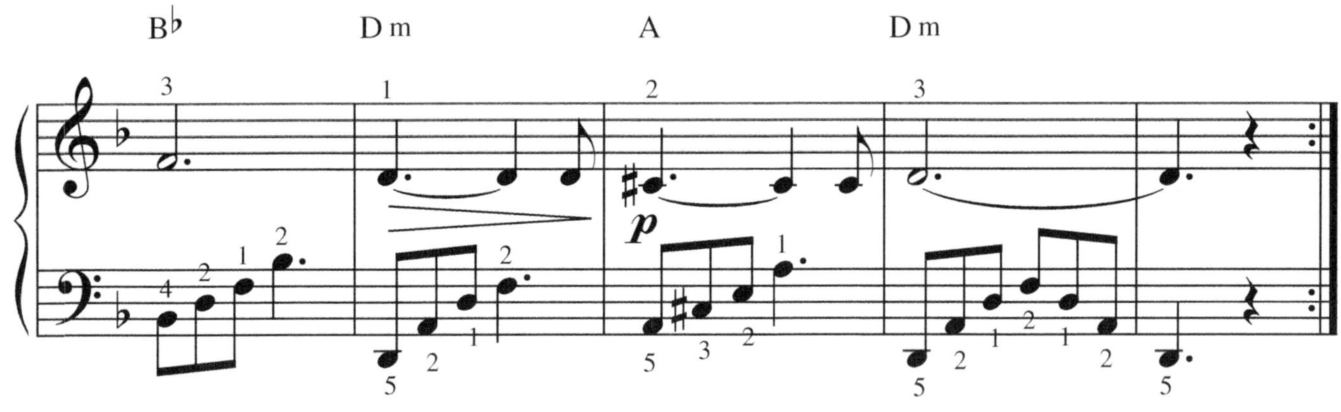

C7 chord (C7)

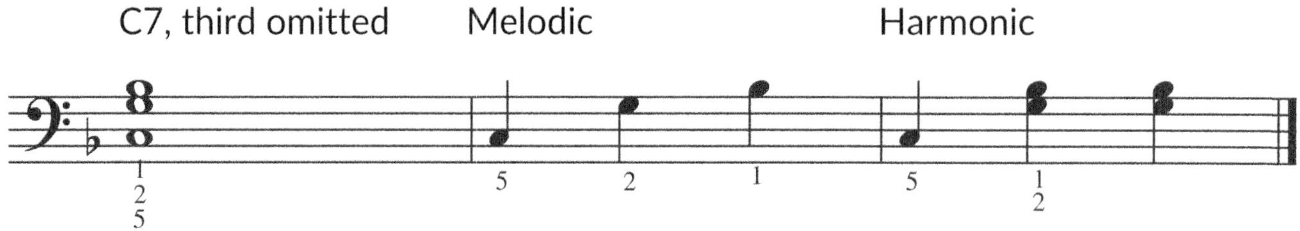

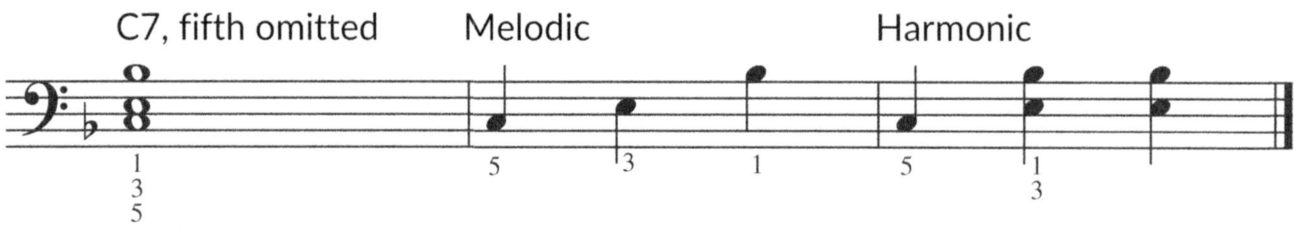

Blow the Wind Southerly

United States (1949)

Unknown composer
Roud 2619
Arr. Bobby Cyr

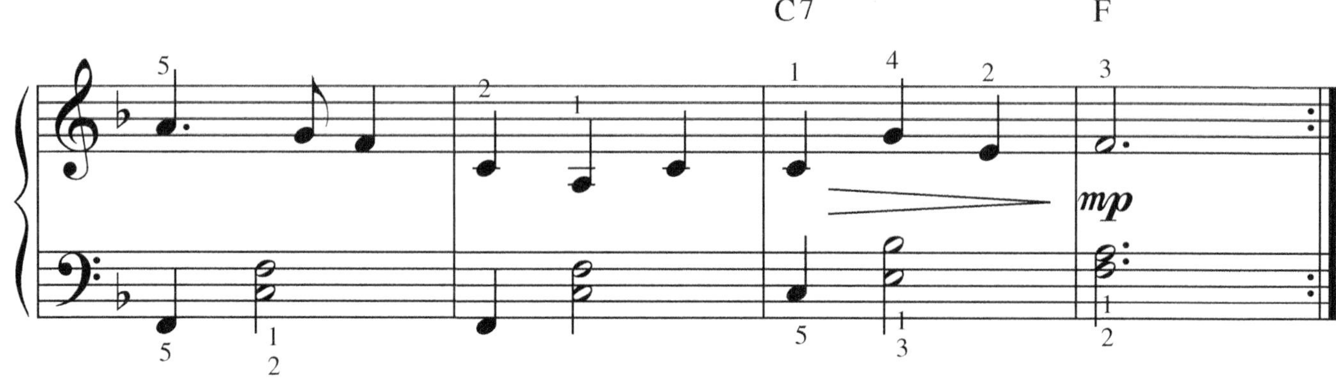

Blow the Wind Southerly

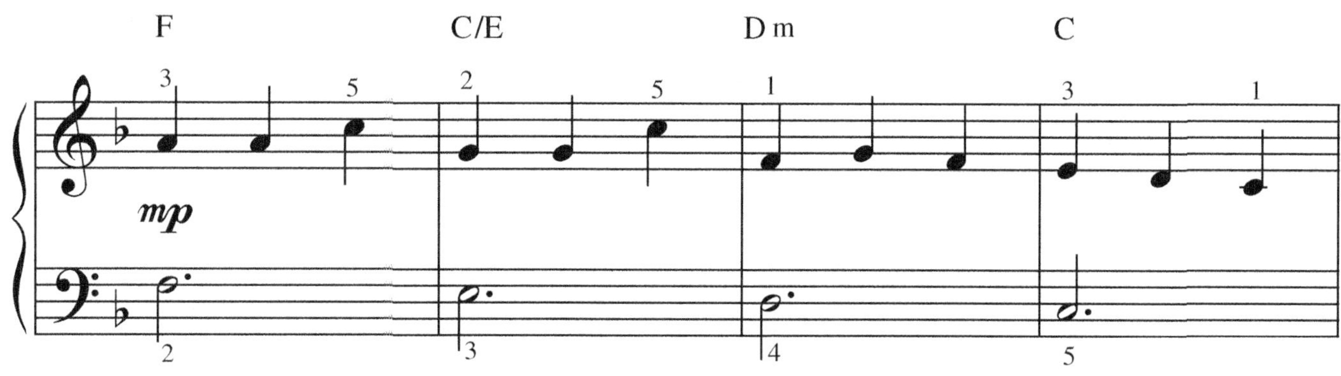

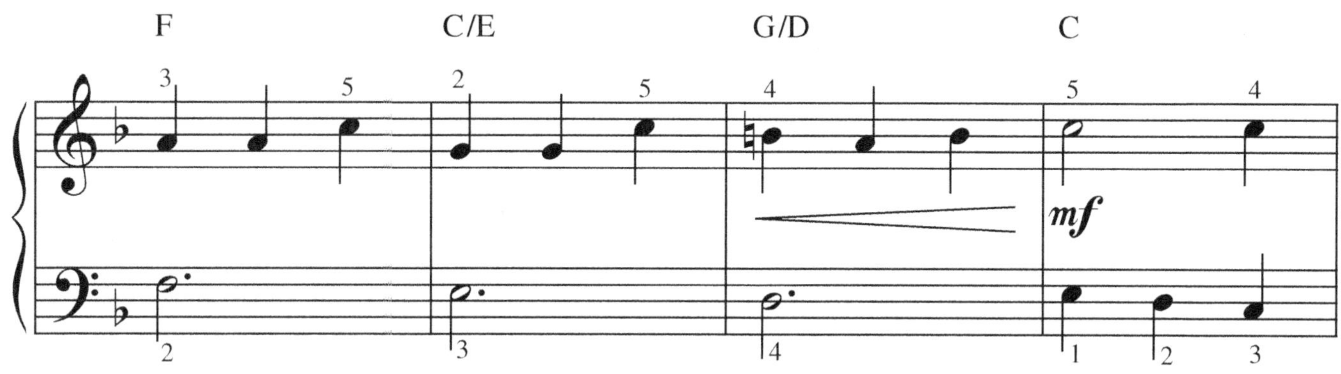

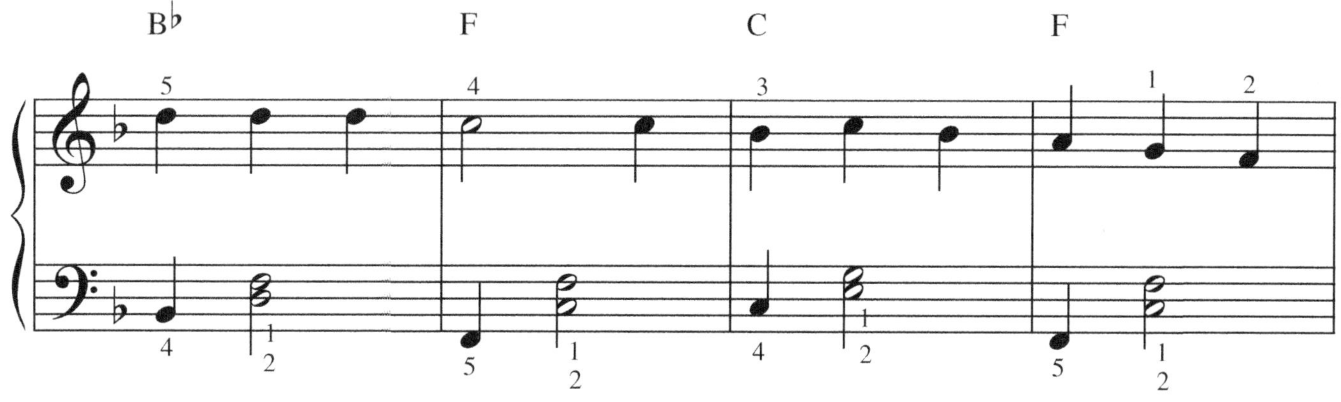

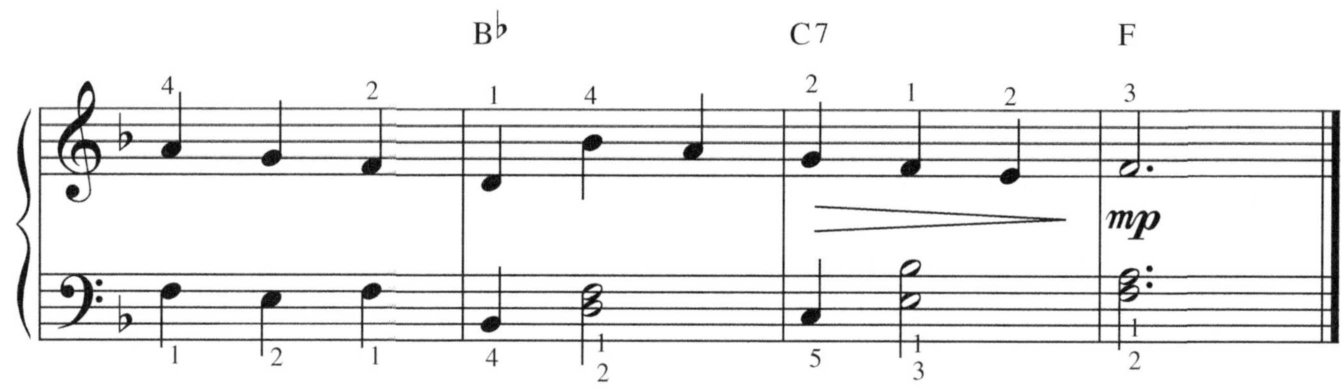

Home on the Range

United States (1873)

Daniel E. Kelley
(1843-1905)
Arr. Bobby Cyr

♩ = 108

F Bb F G7 C F Bb G7 C7 F

mf

Home on the Range

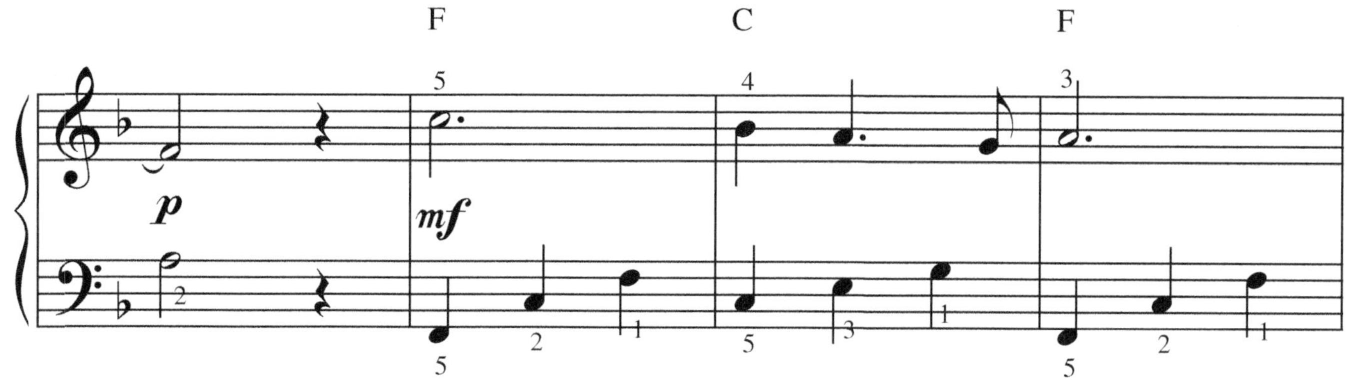

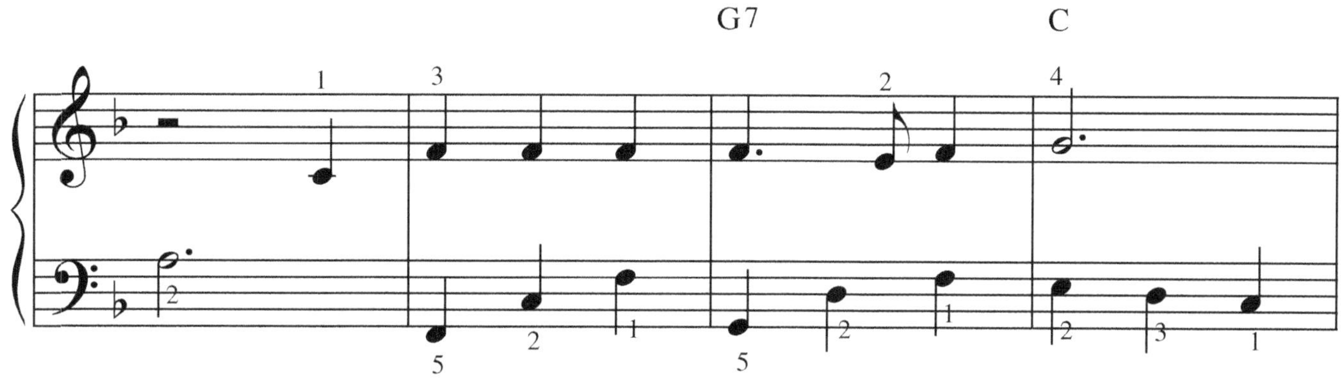

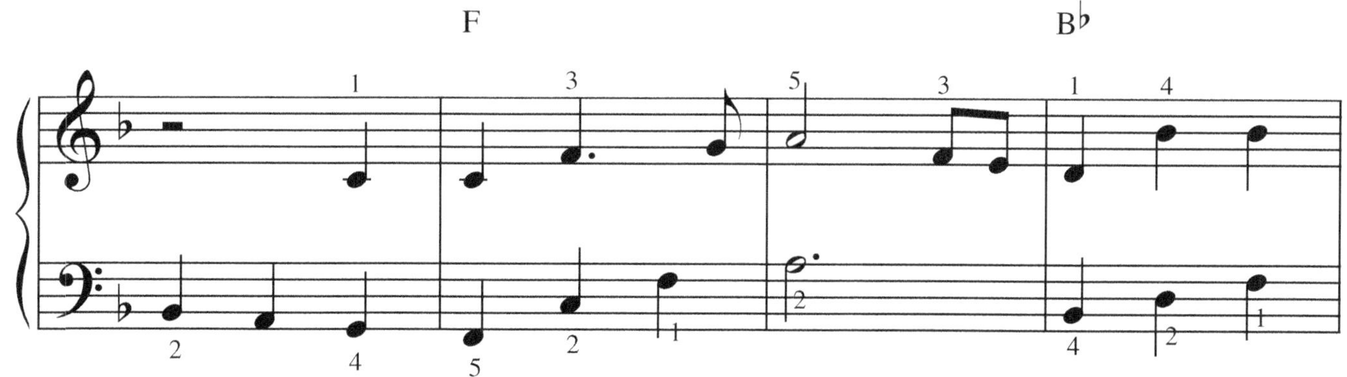

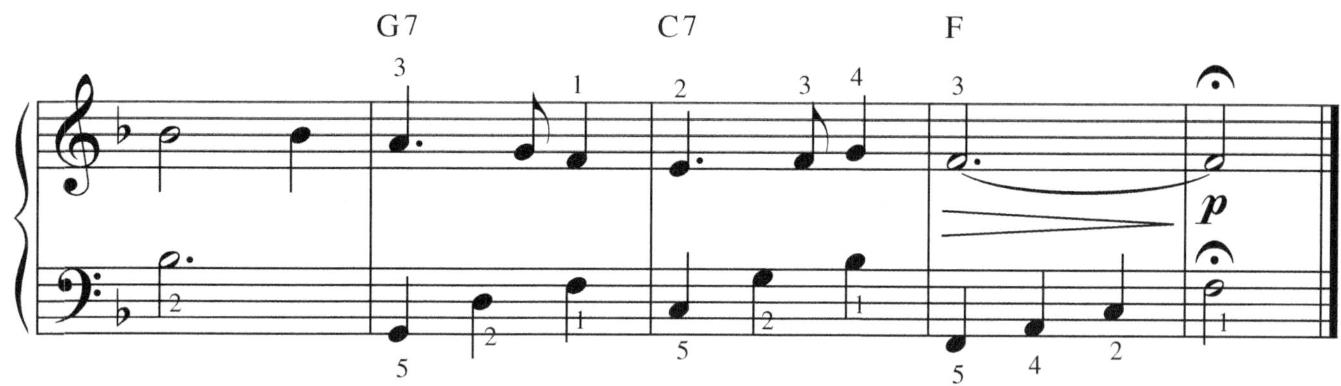

Lorena

United States (1856)

Joseph Philbrick Webster
(1819-1875)
Arr. Bobby Cyr

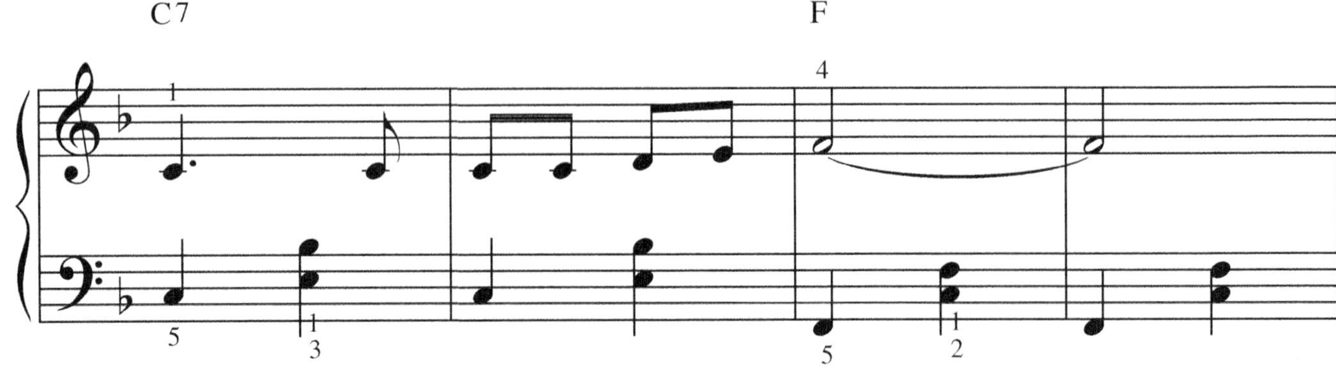

Lorena

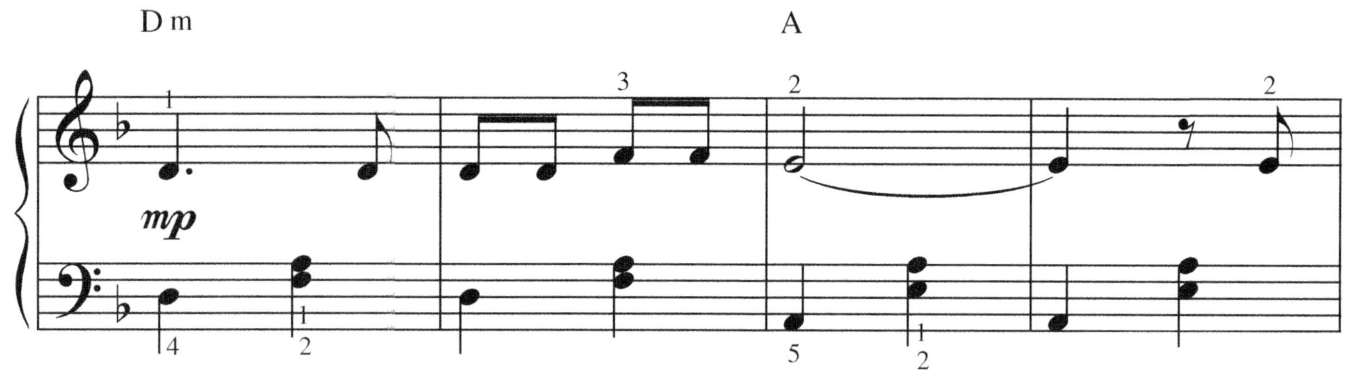

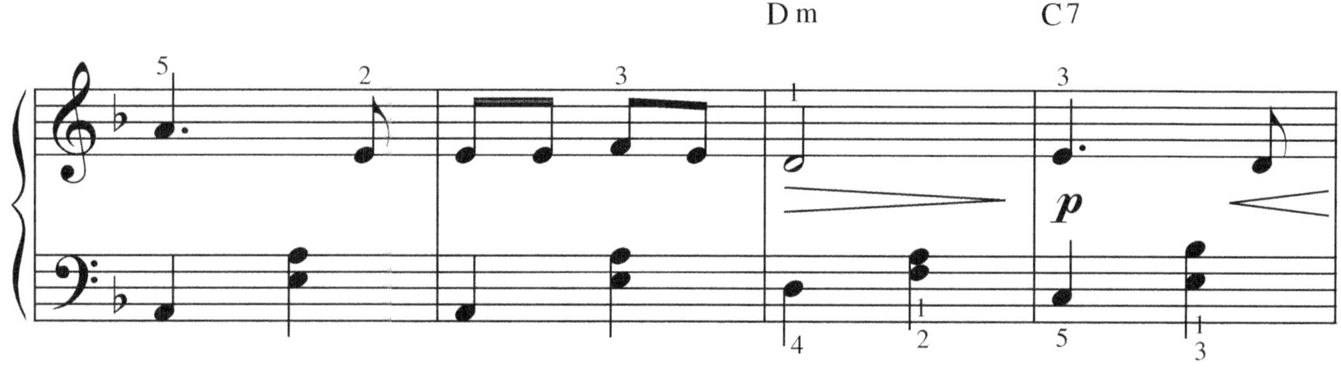

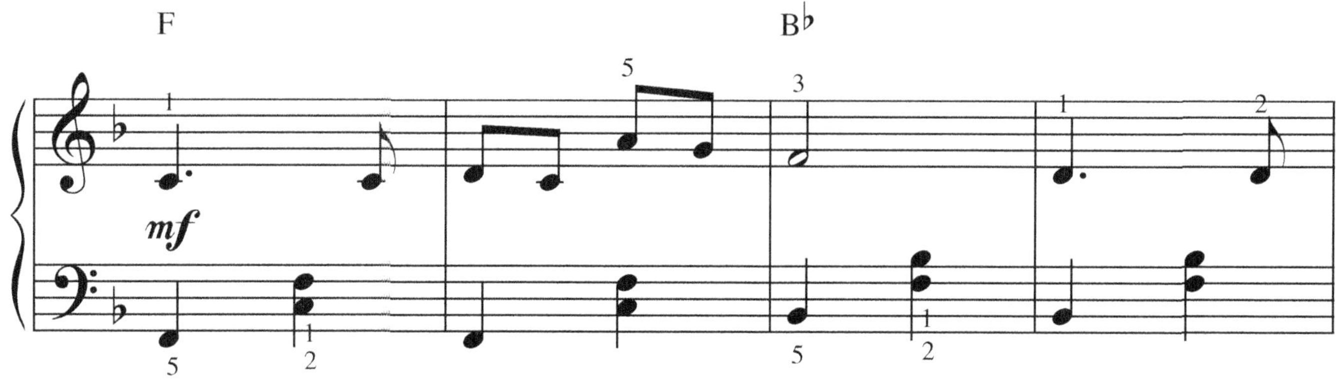

G minor chord (Gm)

Gm Melodic Harmonic

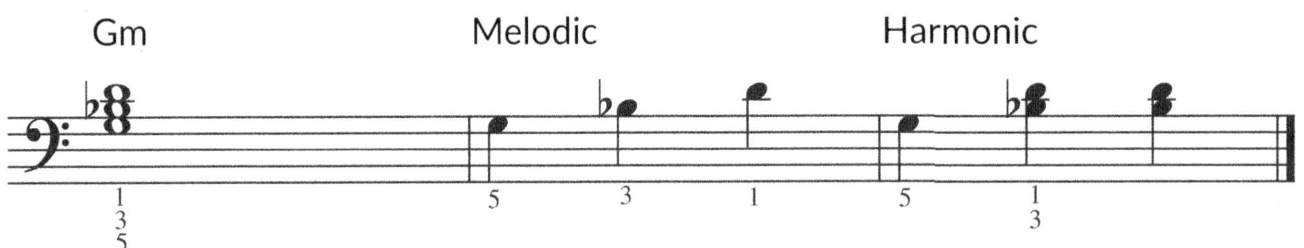

G minor arpeggio (Gm)

Gm (root position) Gm (with the third one octave higher)

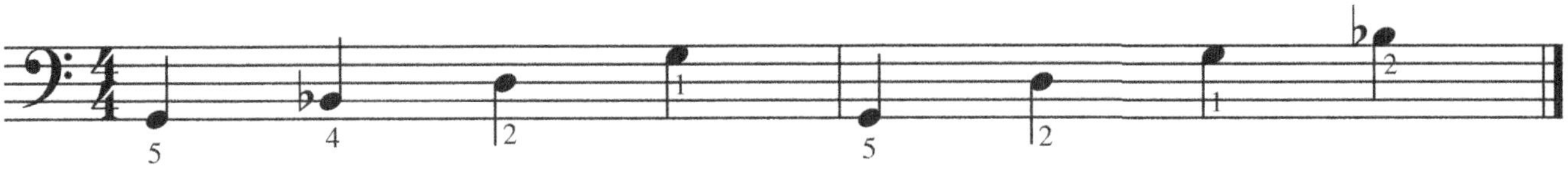

The Skye Boat Song

Scotland

Unknown composer
Roud 3772
Arr. Bobby Cyr

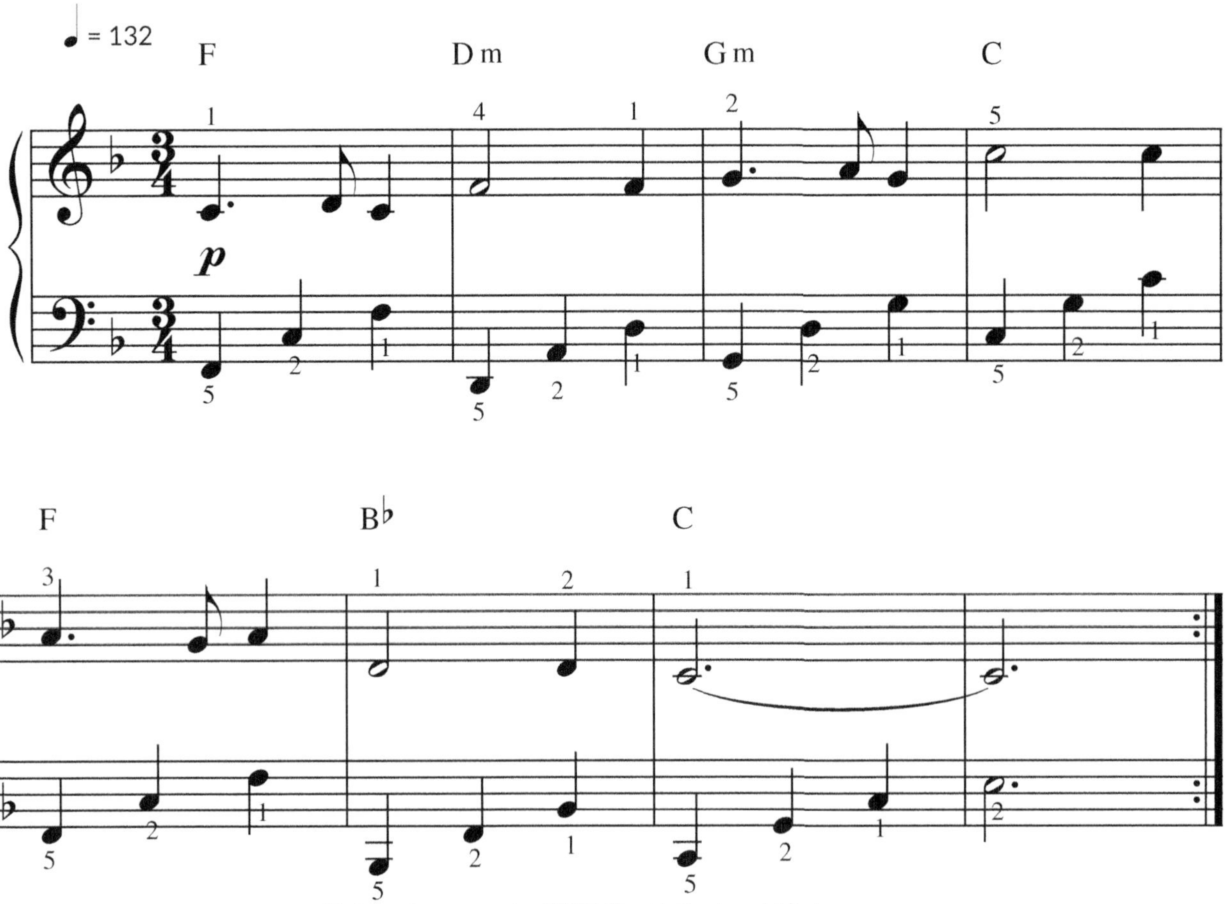

♩ = 132
F
Dm
Gm
C
p
F
B♭
C

The Skye Boat Song

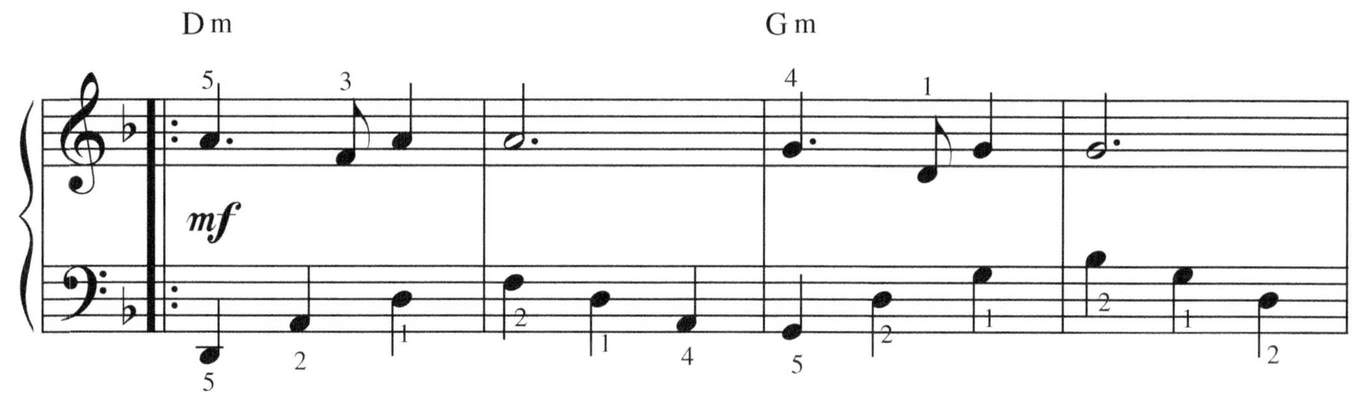

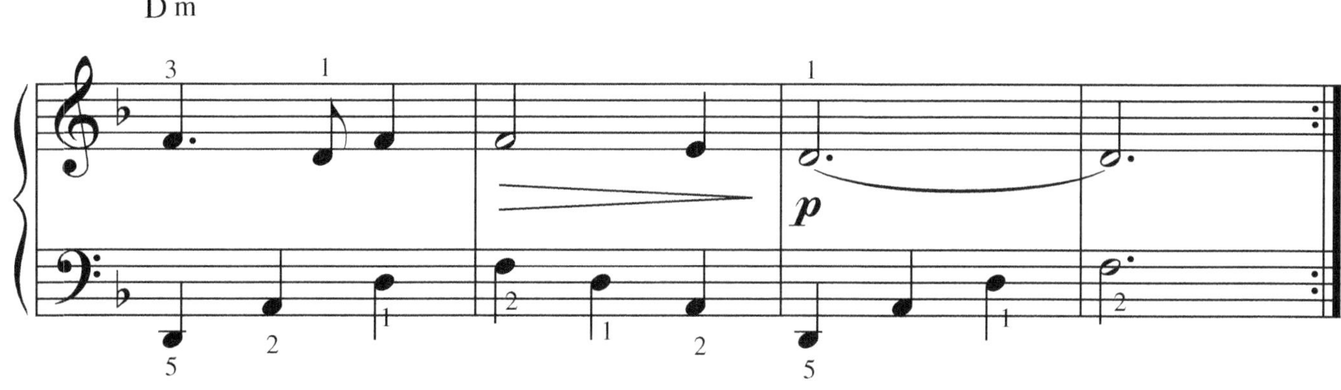

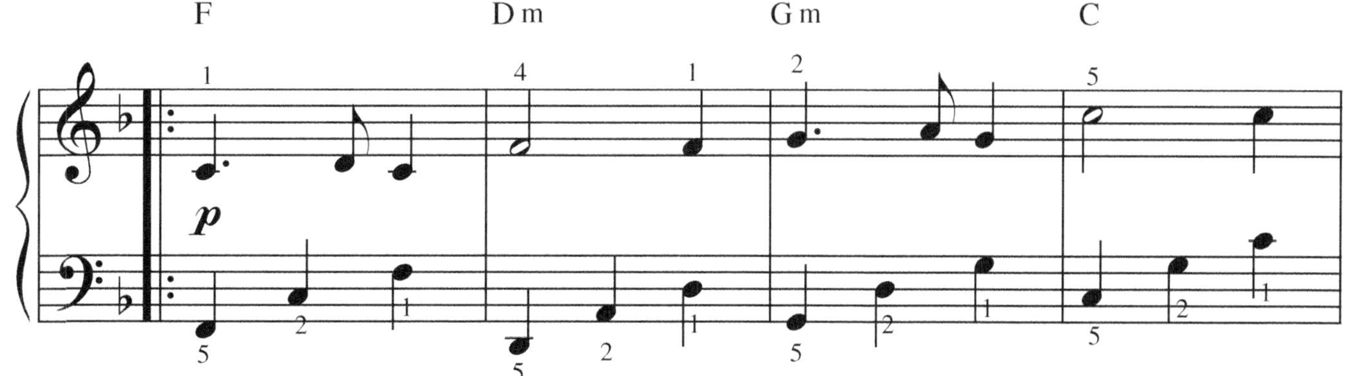

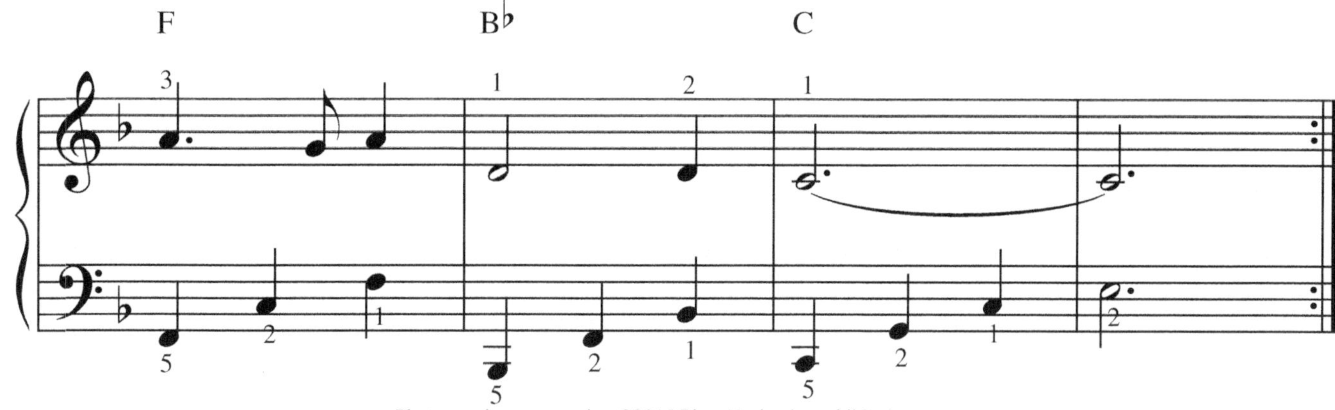

Over the Waves

Sobre Las Olas
Mexico (1884)

Juventino Rosas
(1868-1894)
Arr. Bobby Cyr

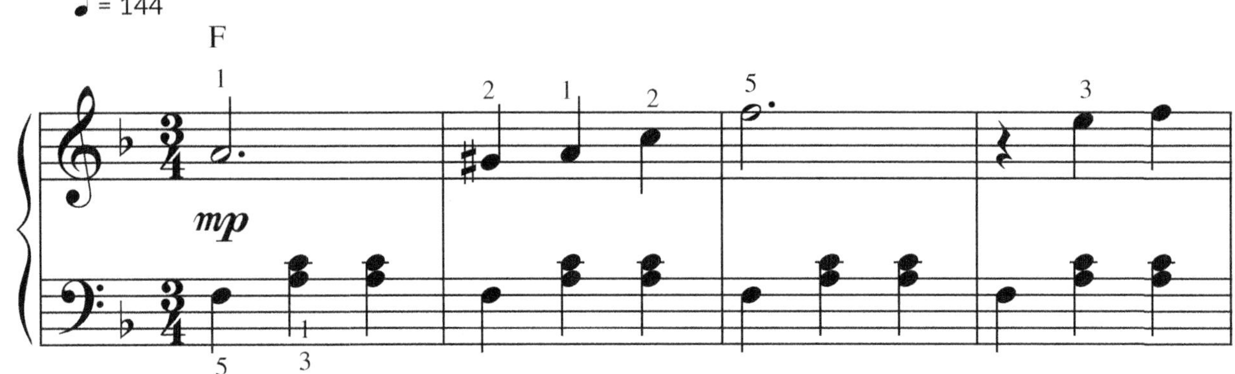

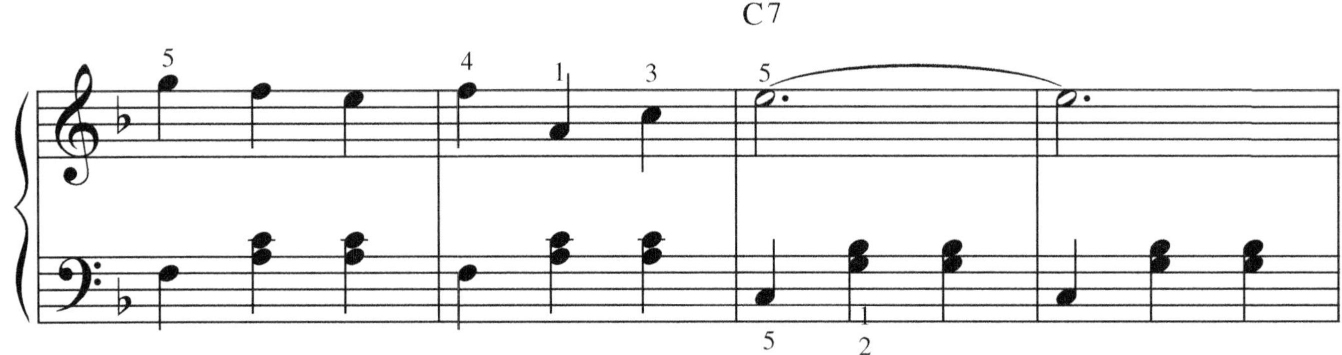

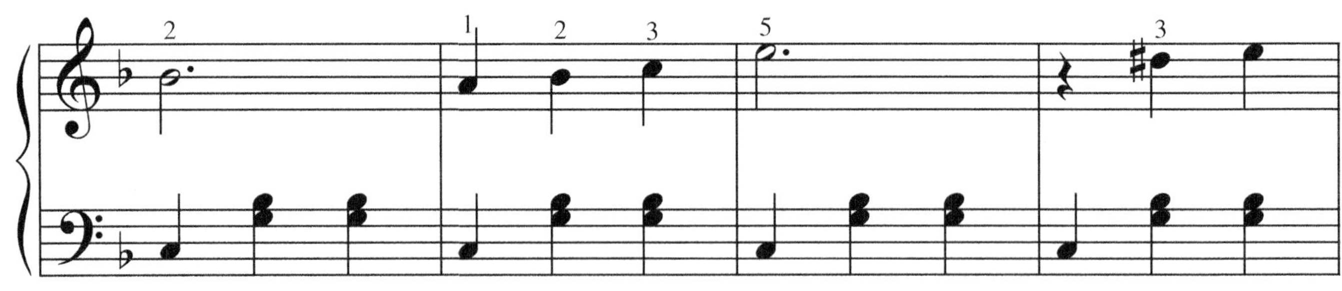

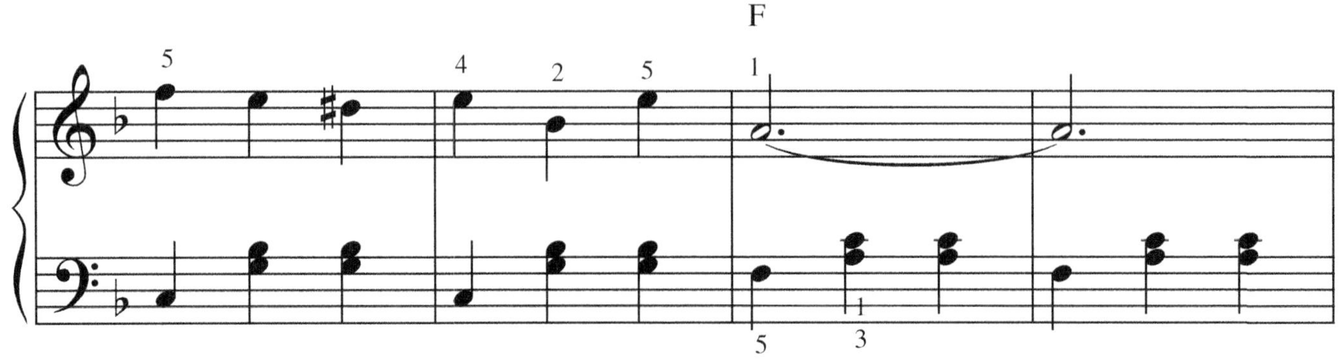

Over the Waves

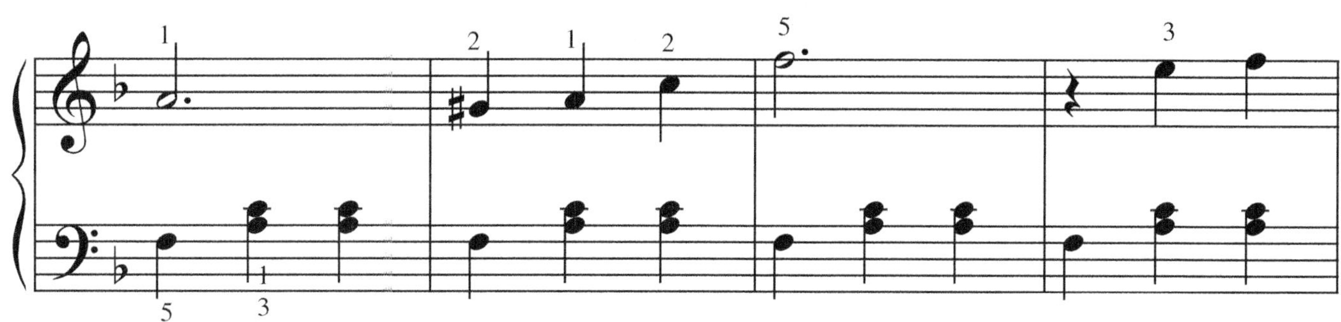

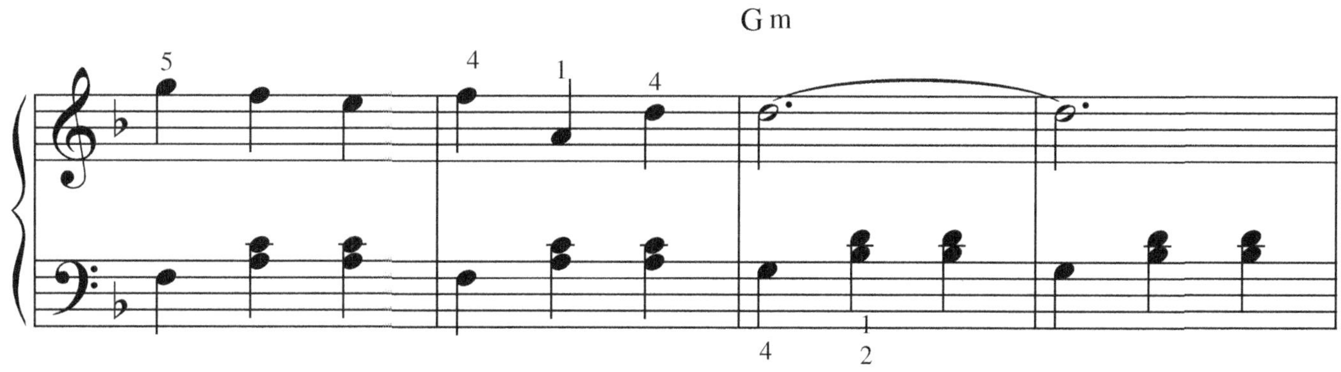

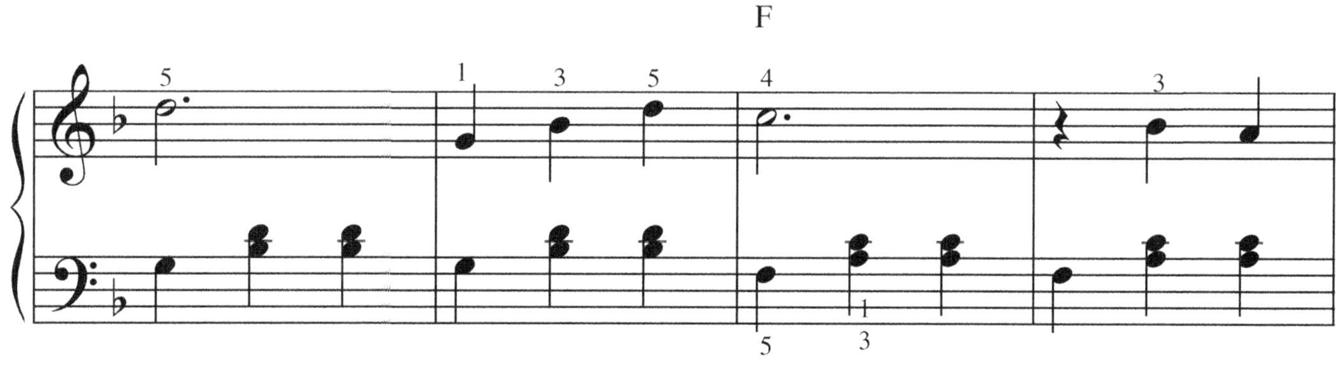

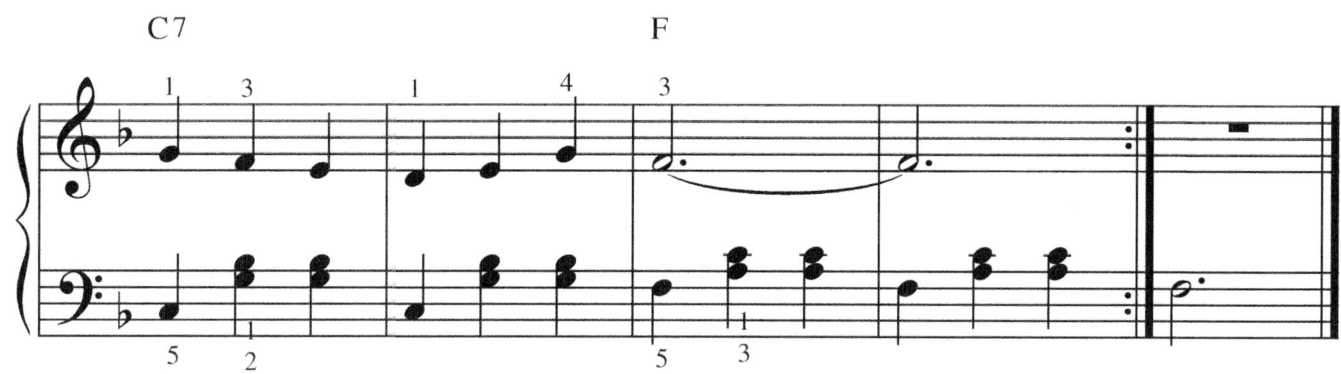

Pleasure of Love

Plaisir d'amour
France (1784)

Jean-Paul-Égide Martini
(1714-1816)
Arr. Bobby Cyr

♩. = 52

F C F B♭ F

mp

C B♭ A D m G m

F C F B♭

mp

F B♭ F C F

Pleasure of Love

Wellerman

New Zealand (1860)

Unknown composer
Arr. Bobby Cyr

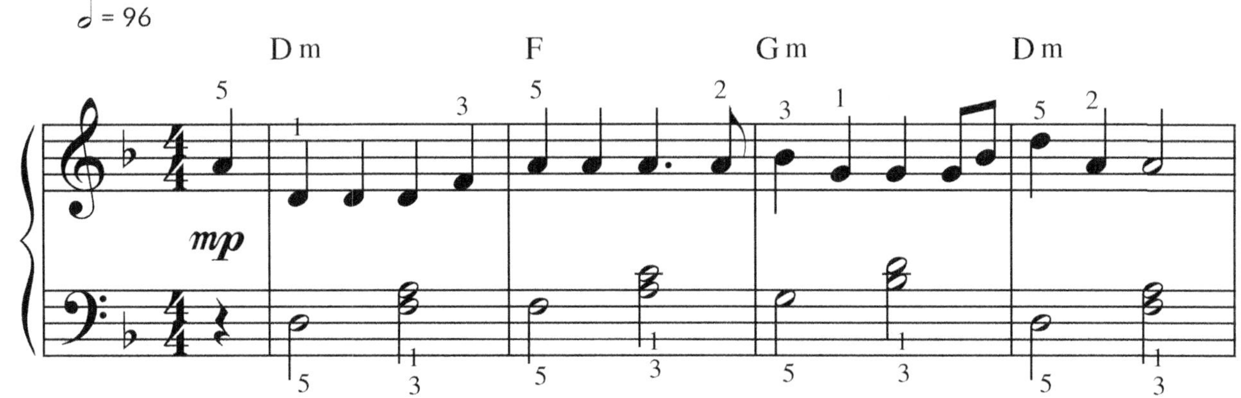

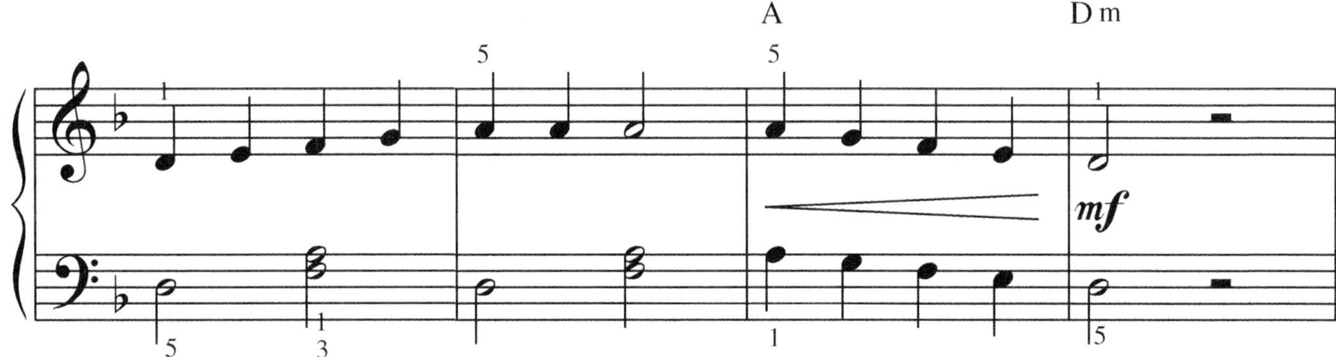

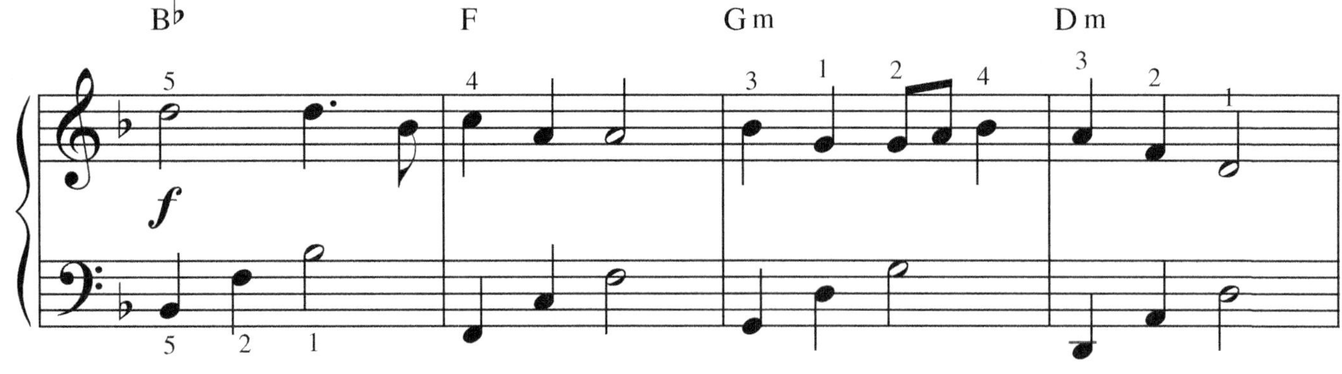

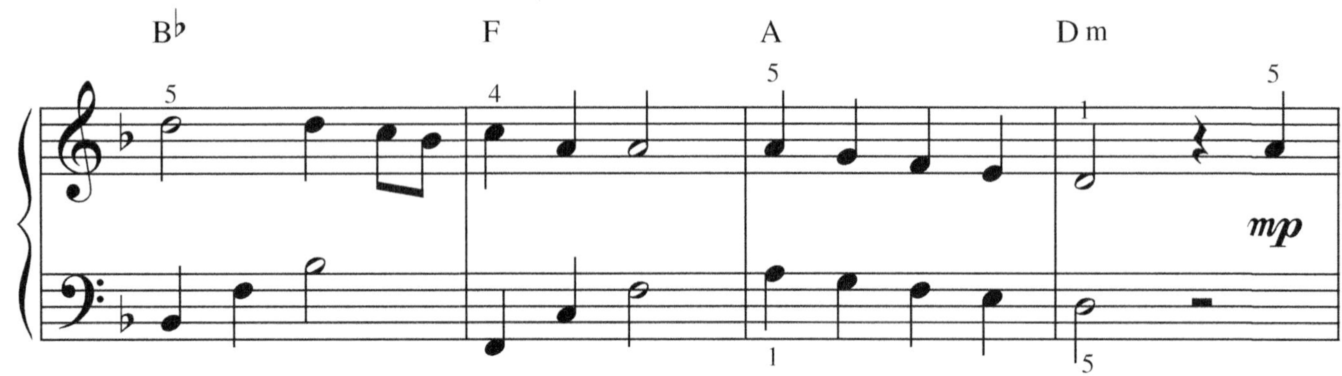

Wellerman

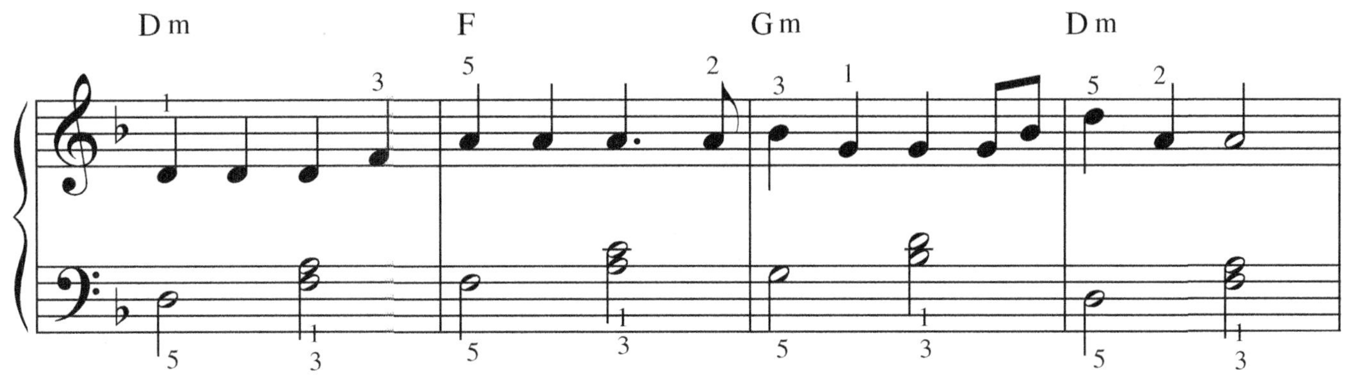

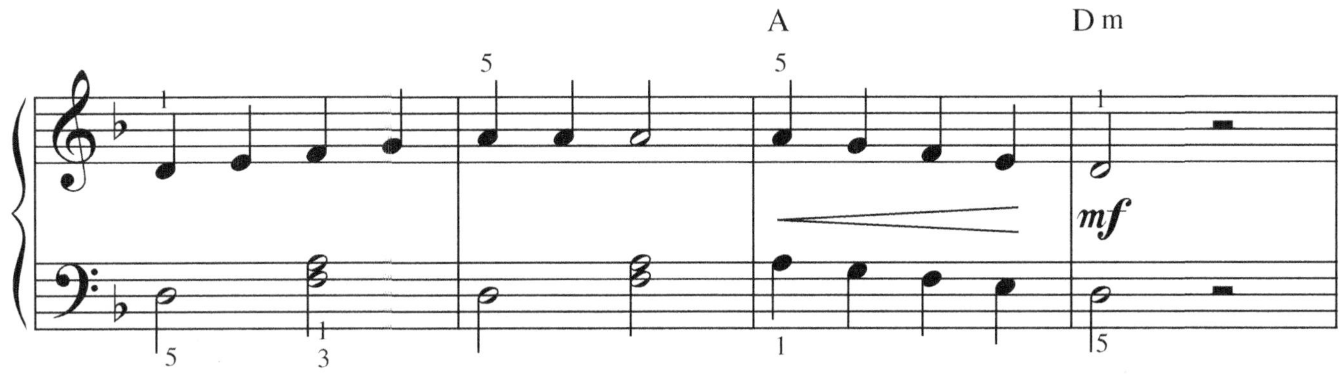

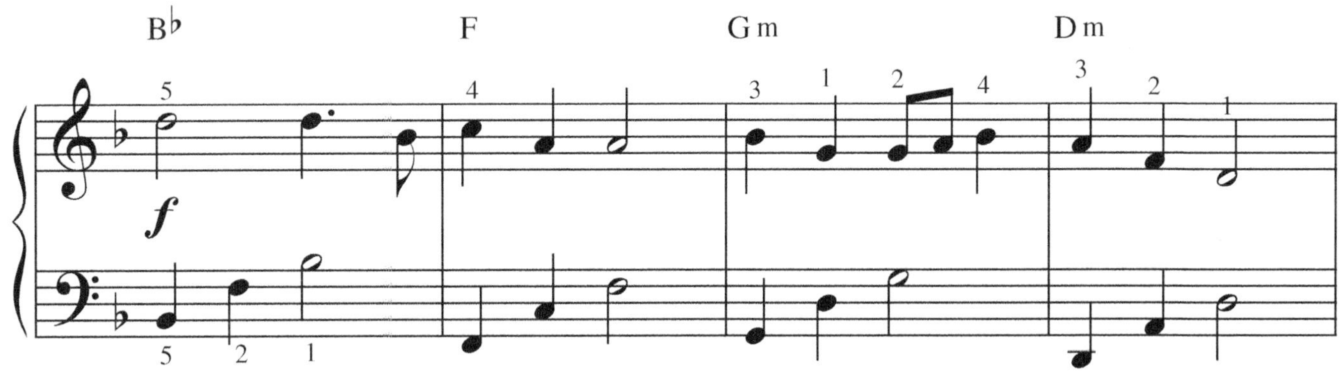

E major chord (E)

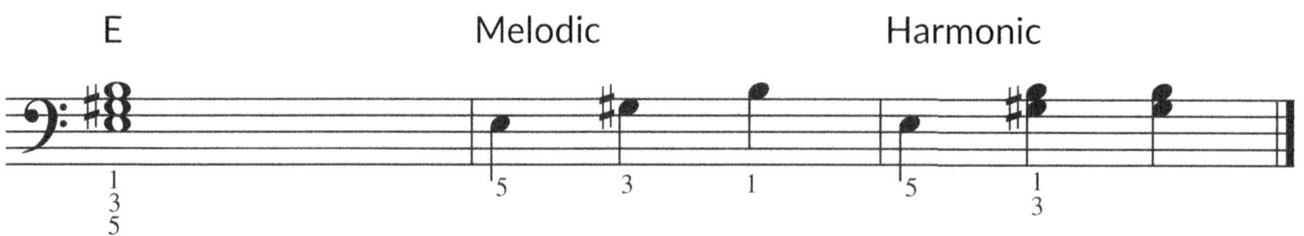

A minor chord with E as the bass (Am/E)

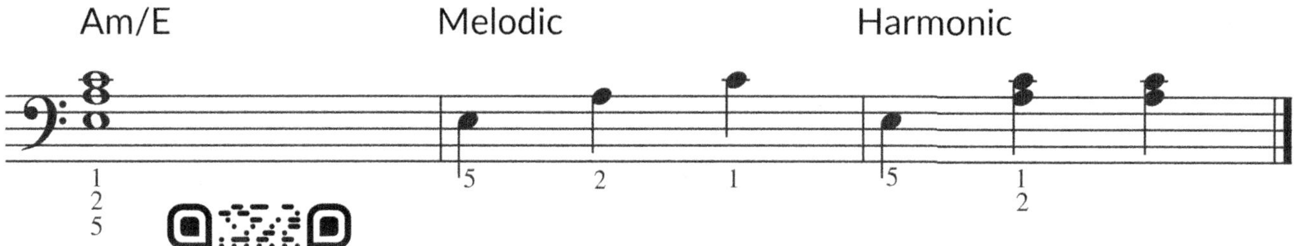

Am/E

Melodic

Harmonic

1 2 5

5 2 1

5 1 2

Kazachok

Ukraine

Unknown composer
Arr. Bobby Cyr

♩ = 100

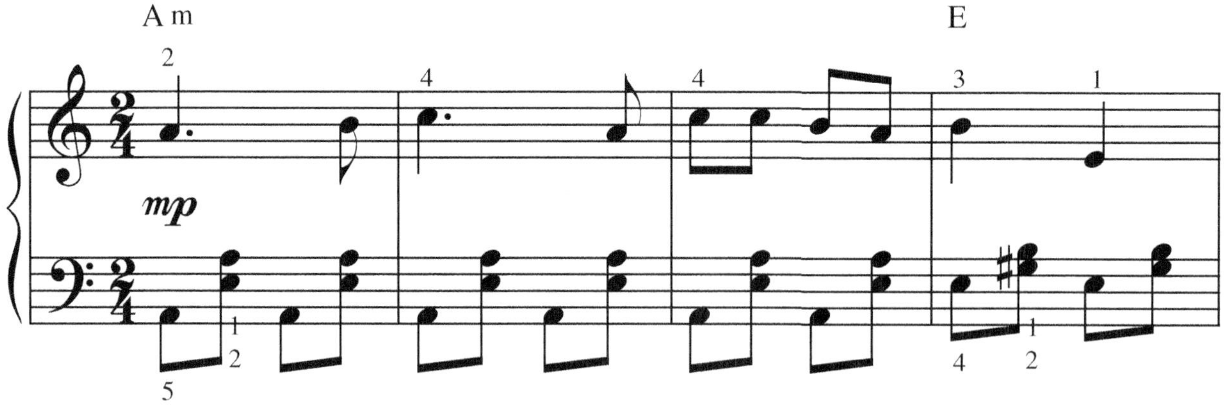

Am

E

mp

Kazachok

Hava Nagila

Israel (1920)

Unknown composer
Arr. Bobby Cyr

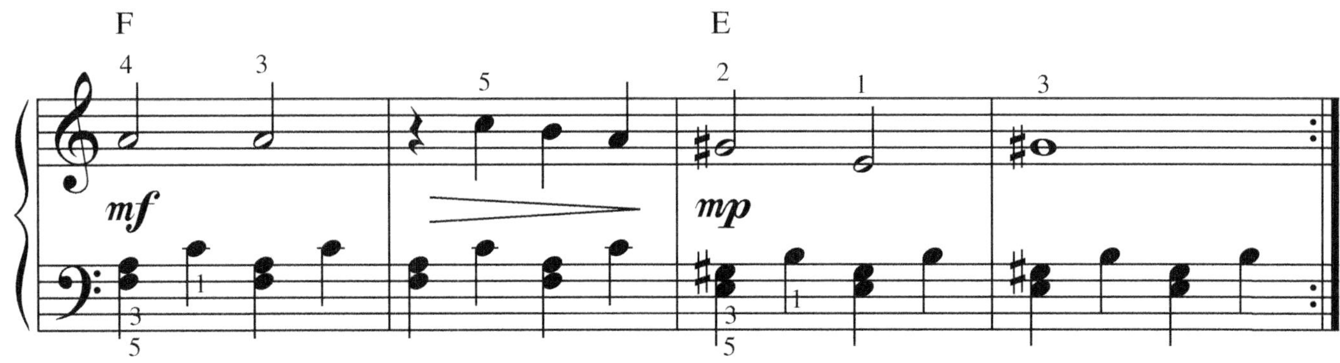

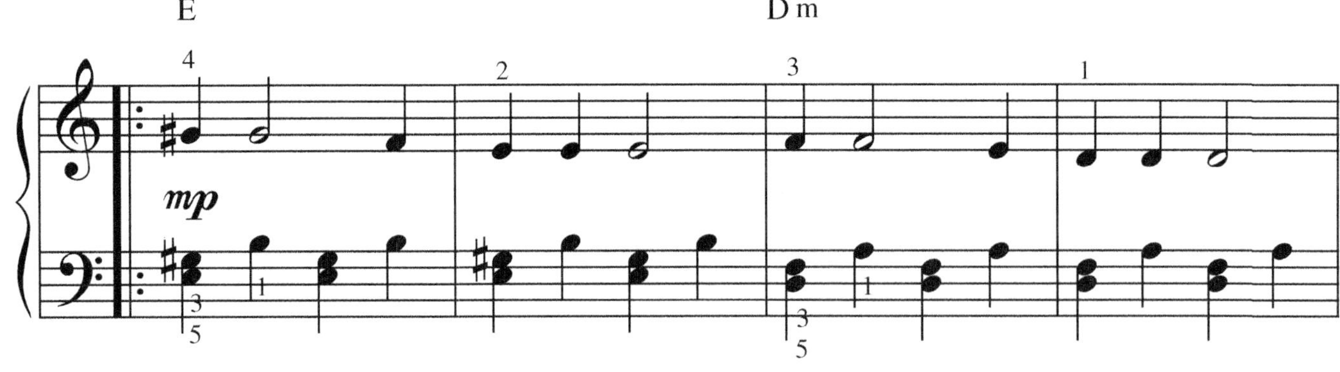

Hava Nagila

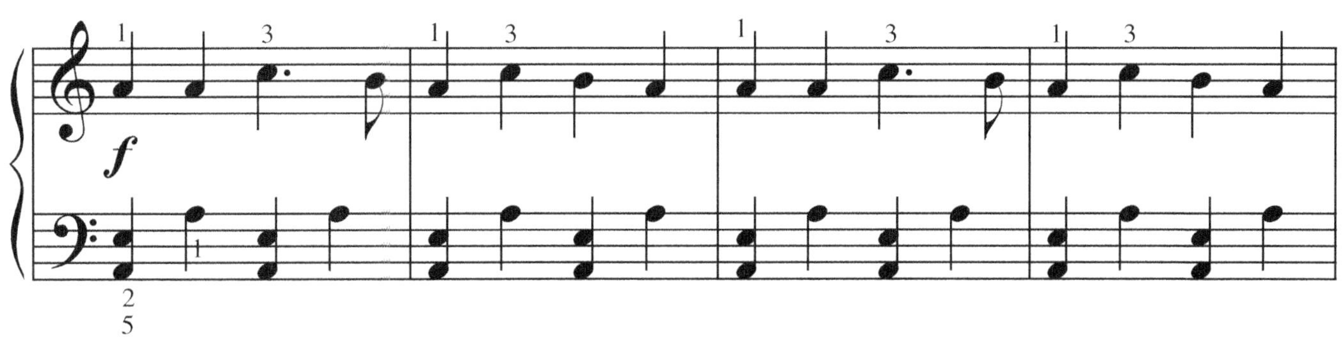

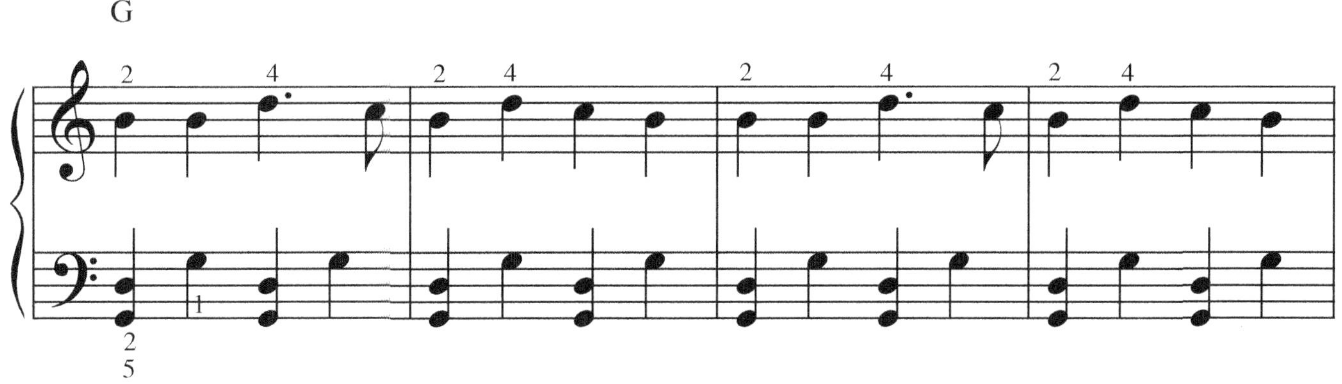

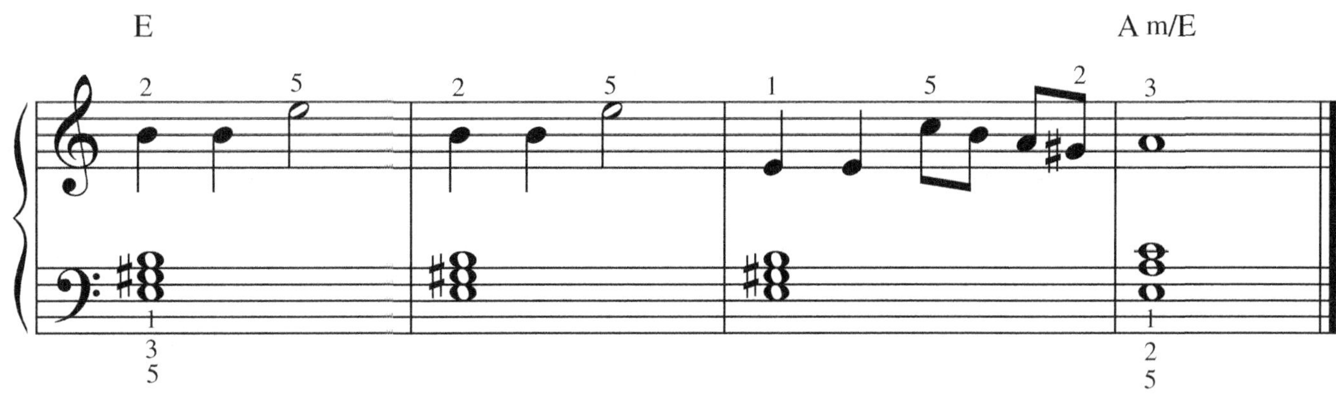

Level 14 pieces

Syncopation

Syncopation occurs when a note is played on a weak beat and held through the following beat.

Exercise: Count the beats out loud while clapping the rhythm.

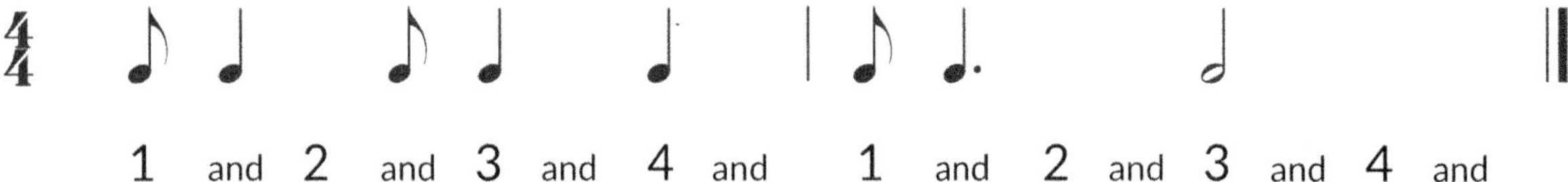

Exercise: See Appendix 1 (page 84)

Tom Dooley

United States (1921)

Unknown composer
Roud 4192
Arr. Bobby Cyr

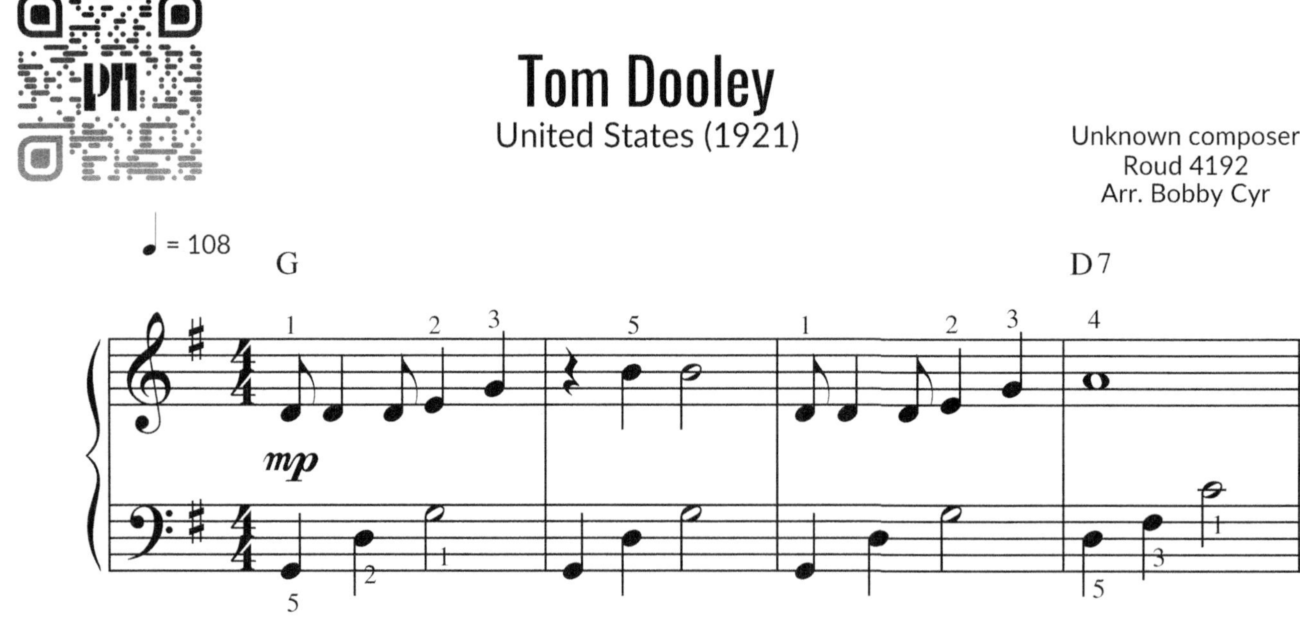

Welsh Lullaby

Suo Gân
Wales

Unknown composer
Arr. Bobby Cyr

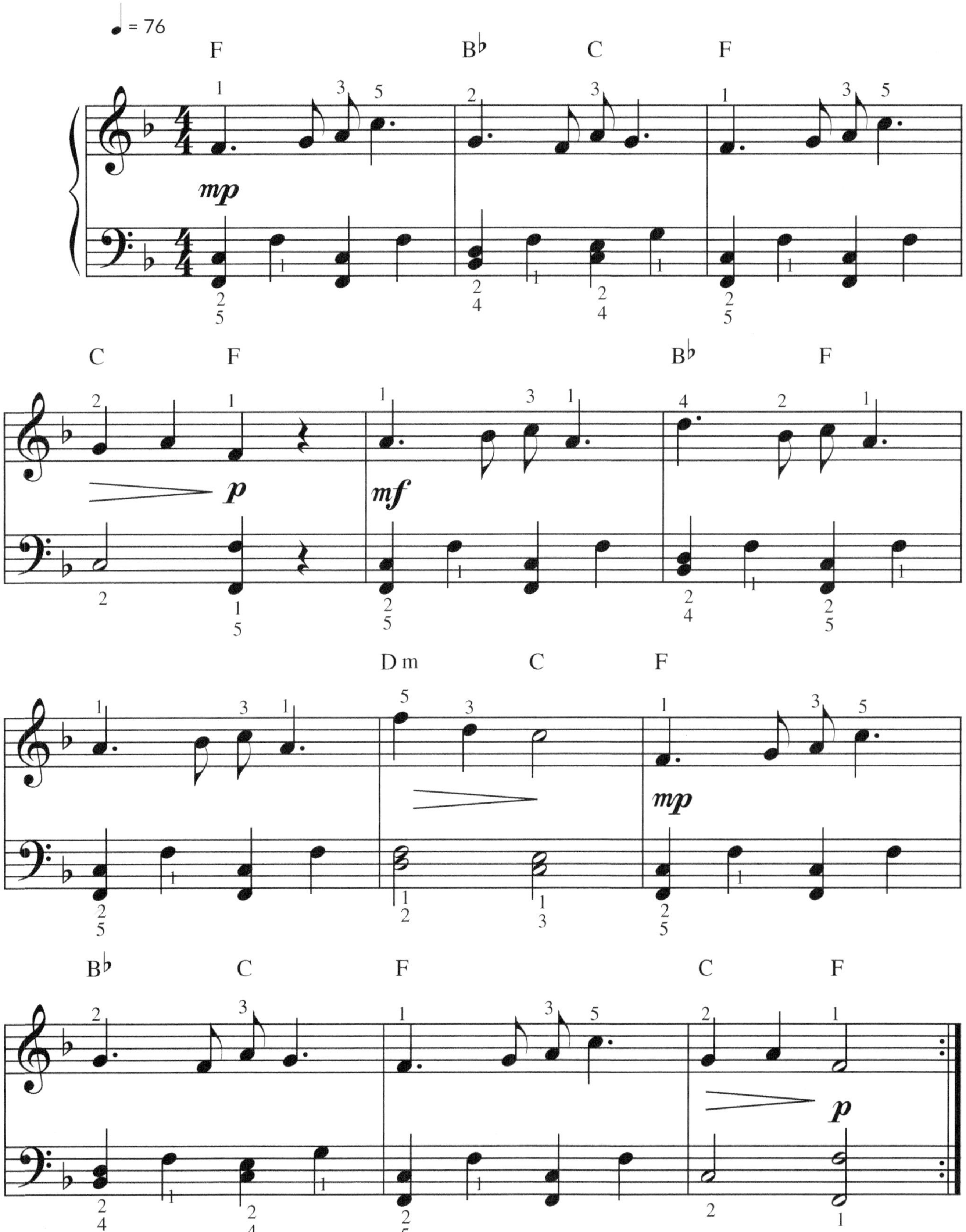

♩ = 76

F B♭ C F

C F B♭ F

Dm C F

B♭ C F C F

This Train

United States (1922)

Unknown composer
Roud 6702
Arr. Bobby Cyr

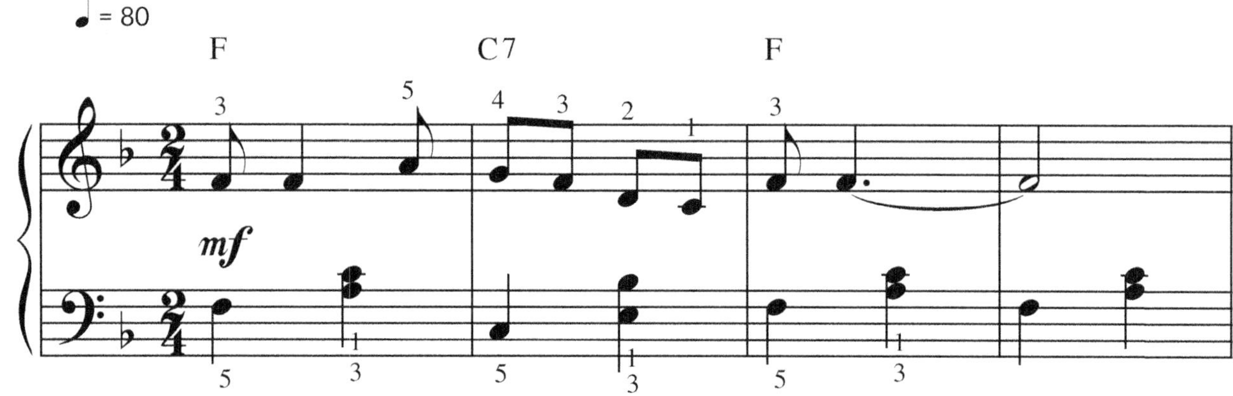

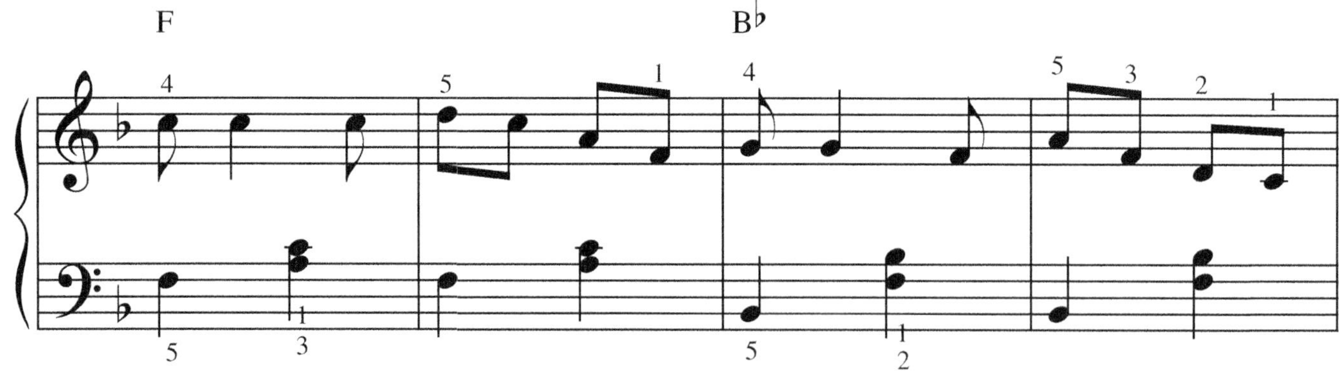

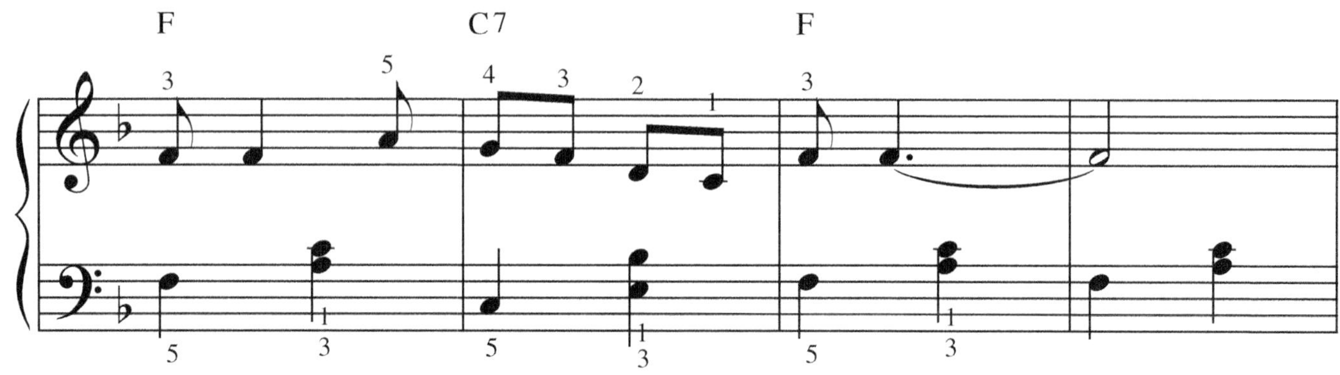

This Train

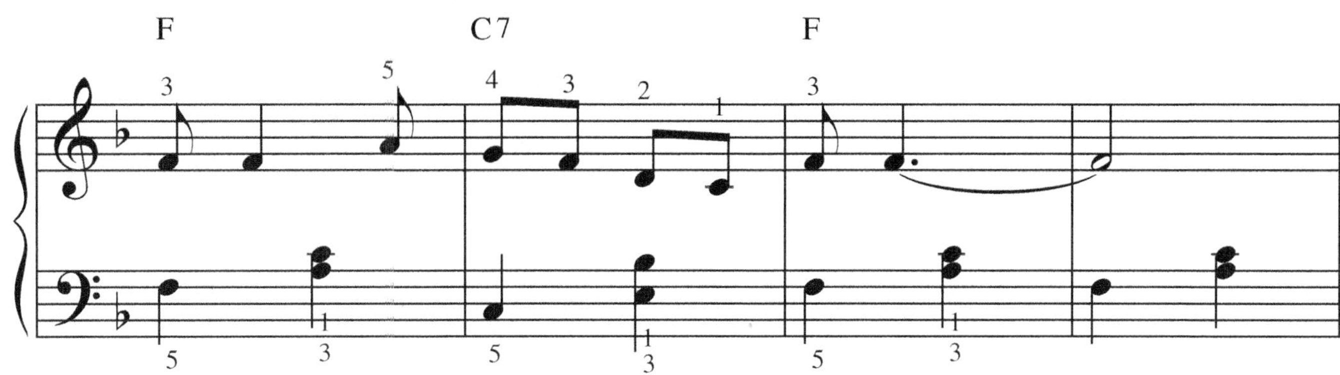

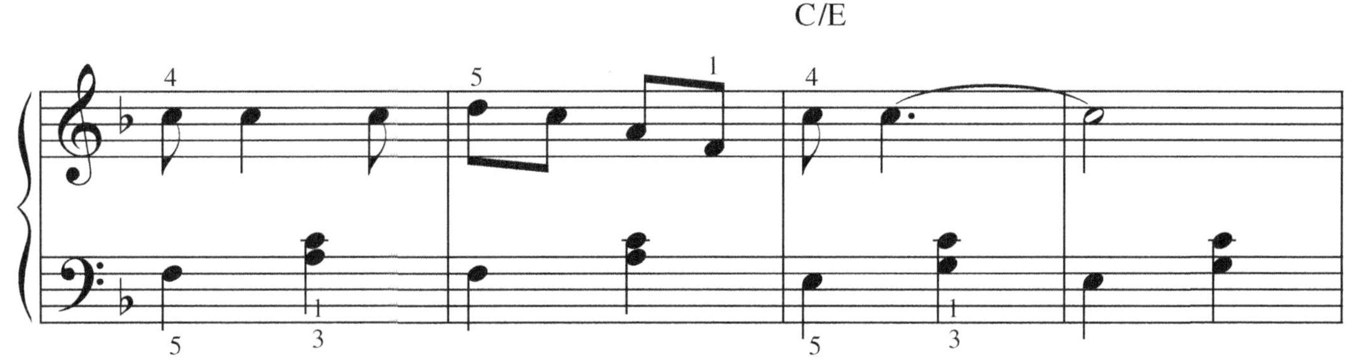

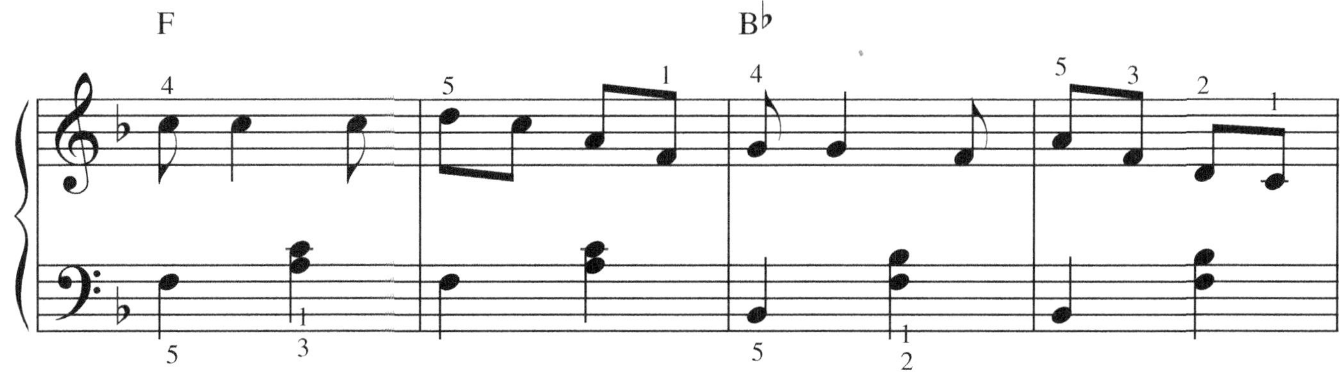

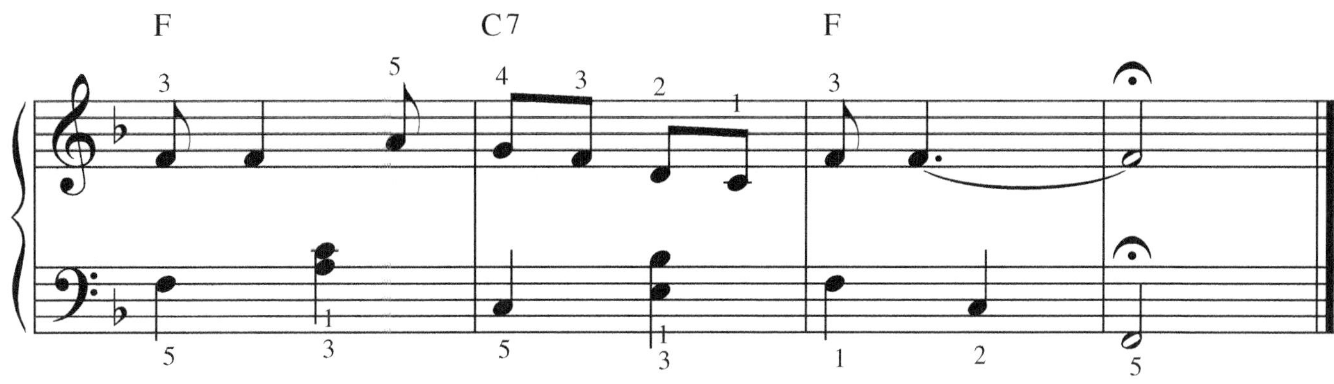

Staccato

A staccato note is played in a shortened and detached manner.

In a piece, staccato is indicated by a dot placed above or below the note head.

Do not confuse a staccato indication with a dotted note.

Examples:

Staccato :
Play short and detached.

Dotted note :
Equal to a quarter note plus an eighth note.

Turkey in the Straw

United States (1820)

Unknown composer
Roud 4247
Arr. Bobby Cyr

Turkey in the Straw

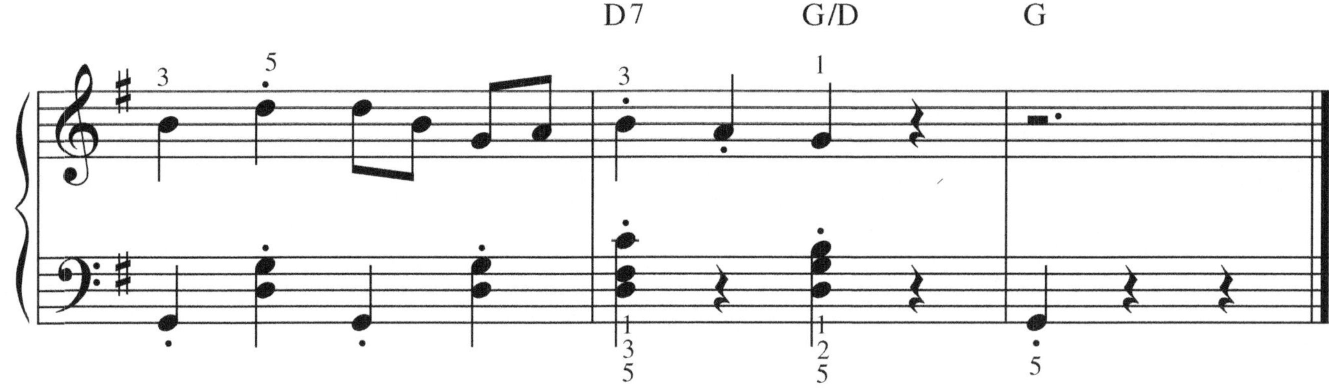

Colonel Bogey March

Great Britain (1914)

Frederick Joseph Ricketts
(1881-1945)
Arr. Bobby Cyr

Colonel Bogey March

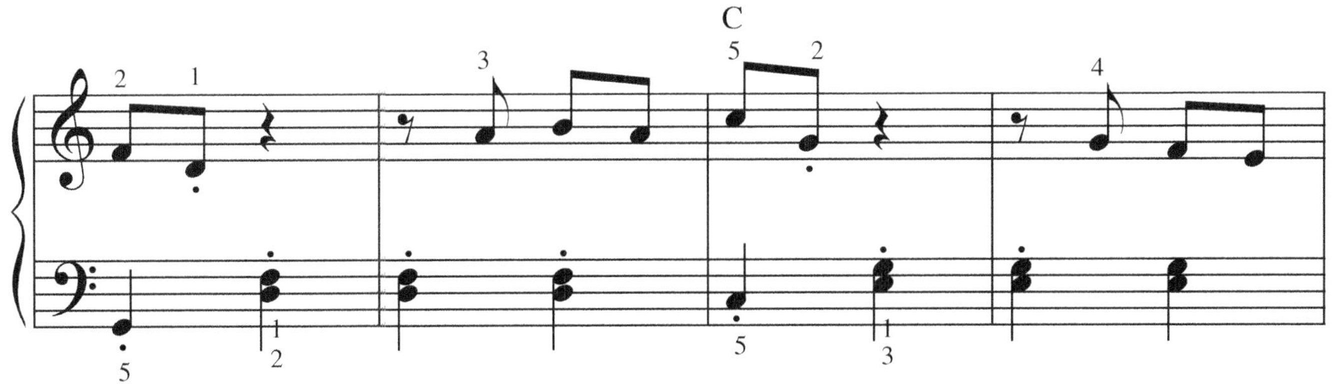

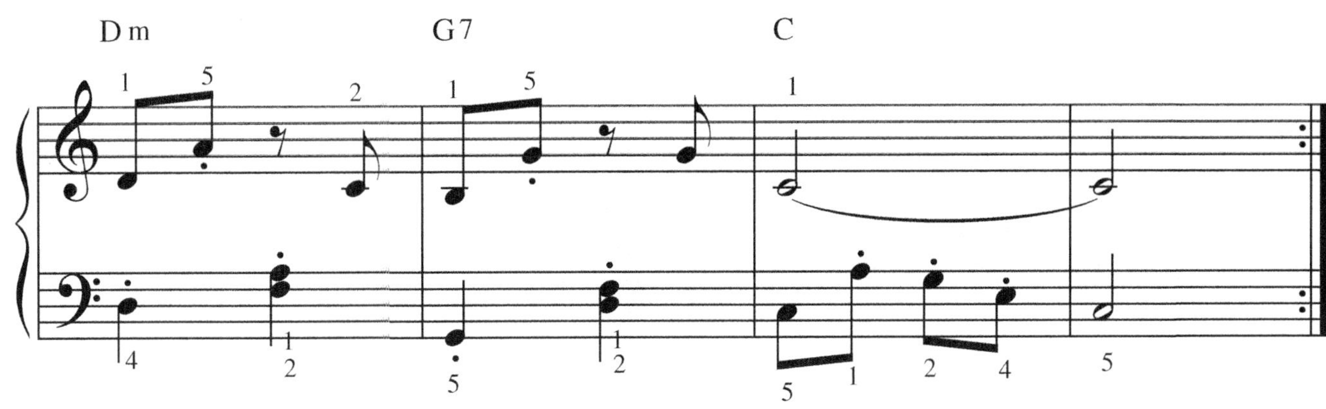

Kalinka

Russia (1860)

Ivan Petrovitj Larionov
(1830-1889)
Arr. Bobby Cyr

Kalinka
A7
Dm
mf
A7
Dm
f
p
C
F
C7
F
C7
F
mp
C7
F
C7
B♭
Gm
C7
F/C
F
p

Daisy Bell

United States (1892)

Frank Dean
(1857–1922)
Arr. Bobby Cyr

♩ = 144

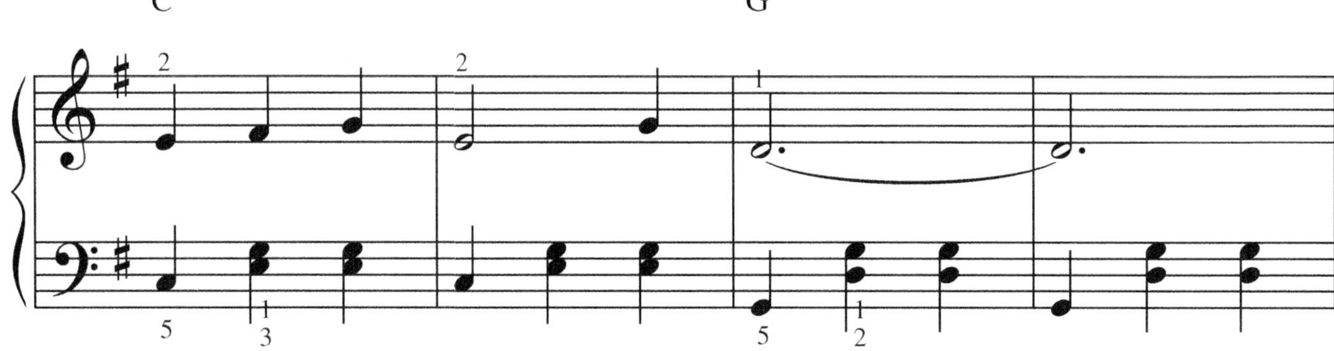

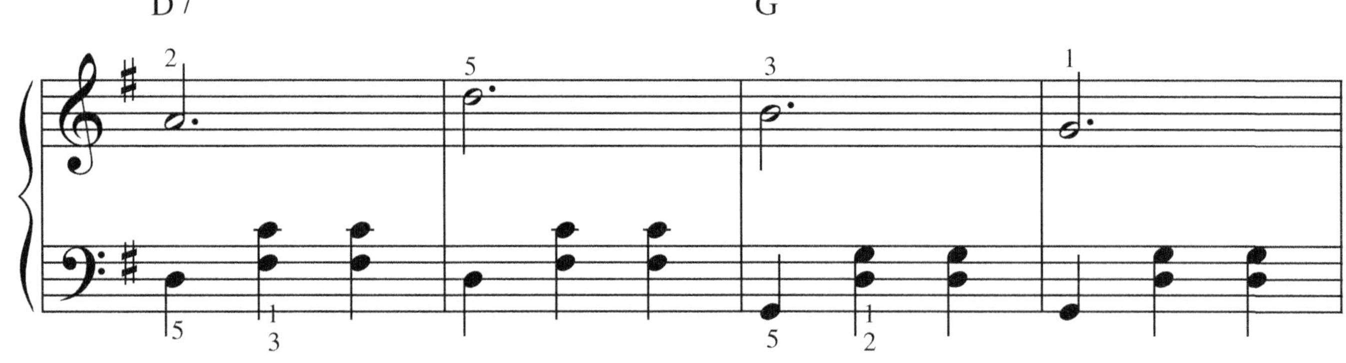

Daisy Bell

G

C G

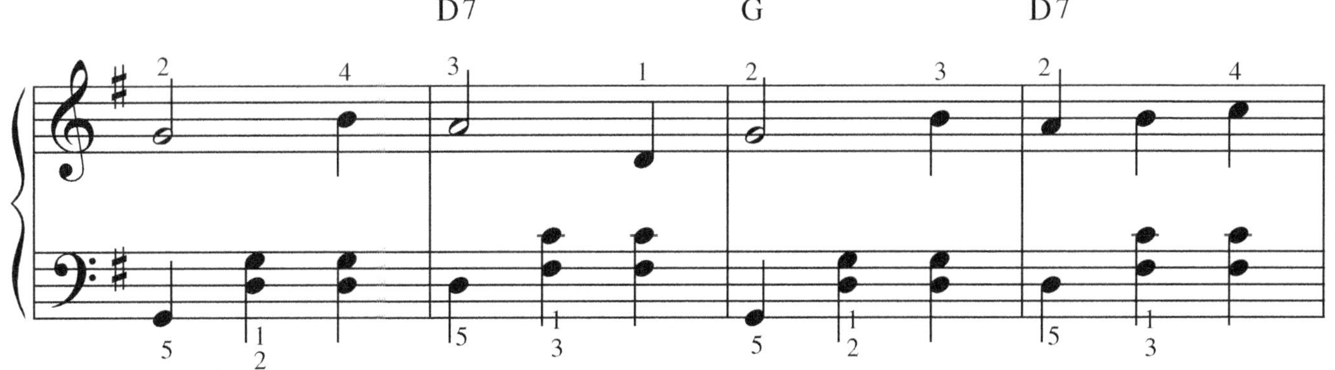

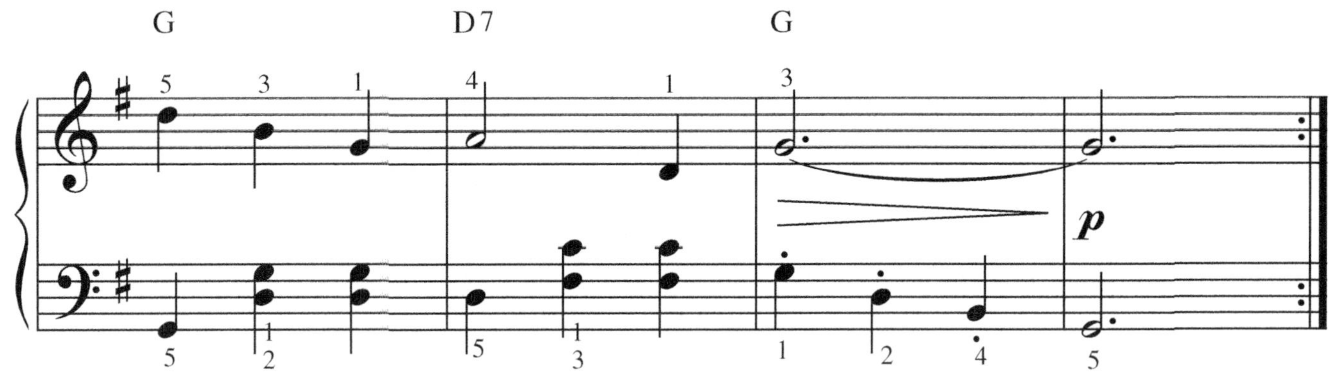

Tumbalalaika

Russia

Unknown composer
Arr. Bobby Cyr

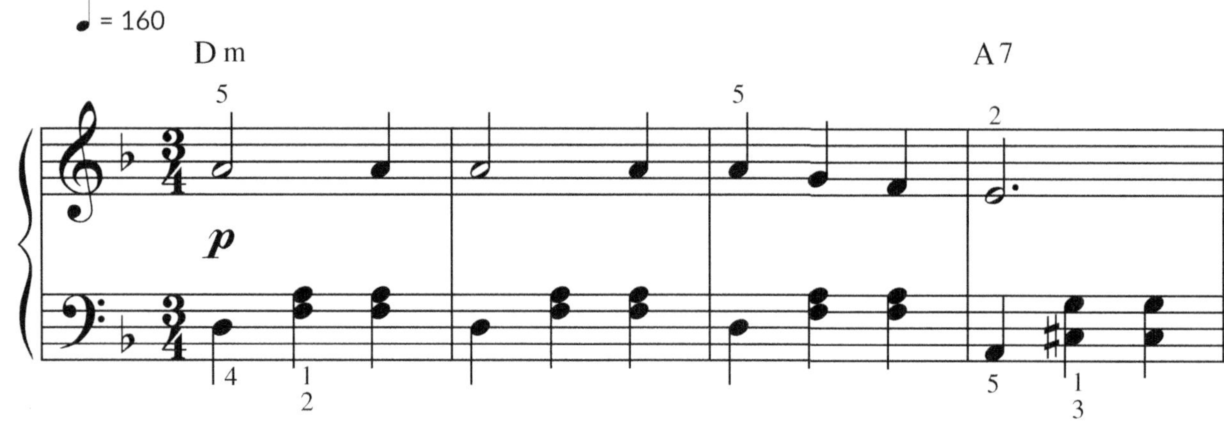

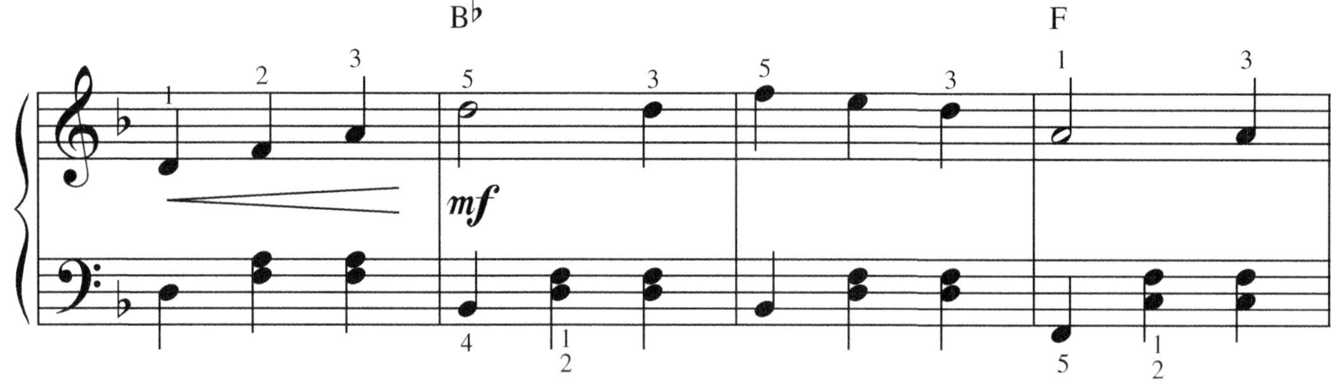

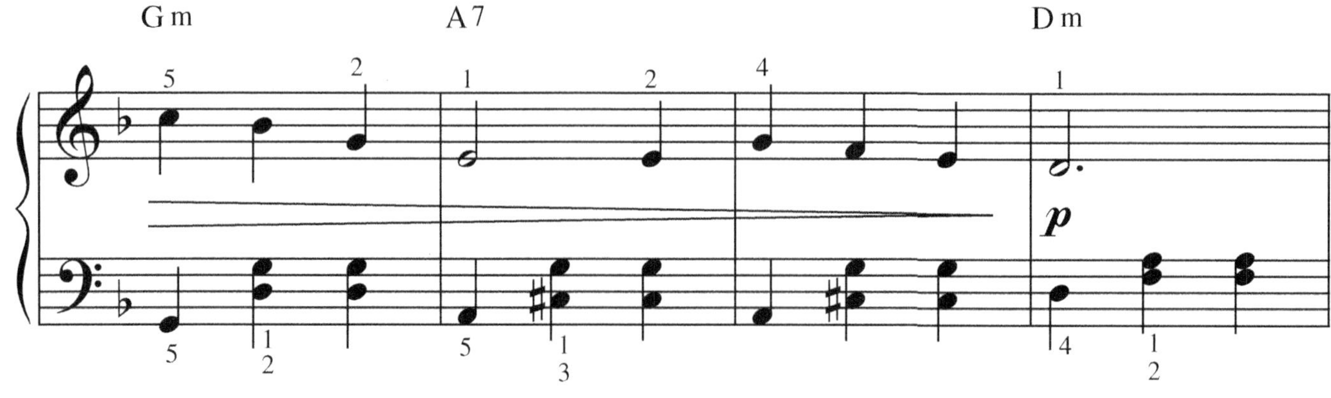

Tumbalalaika

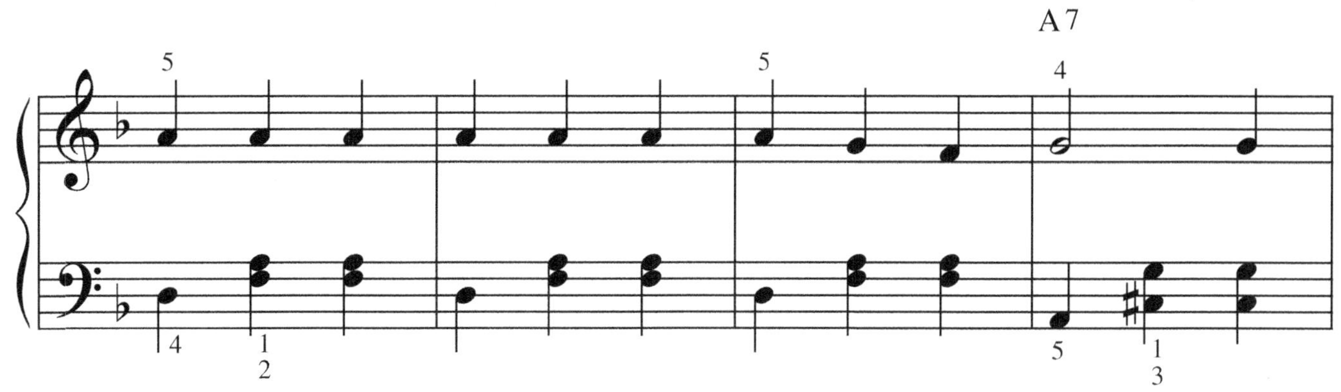

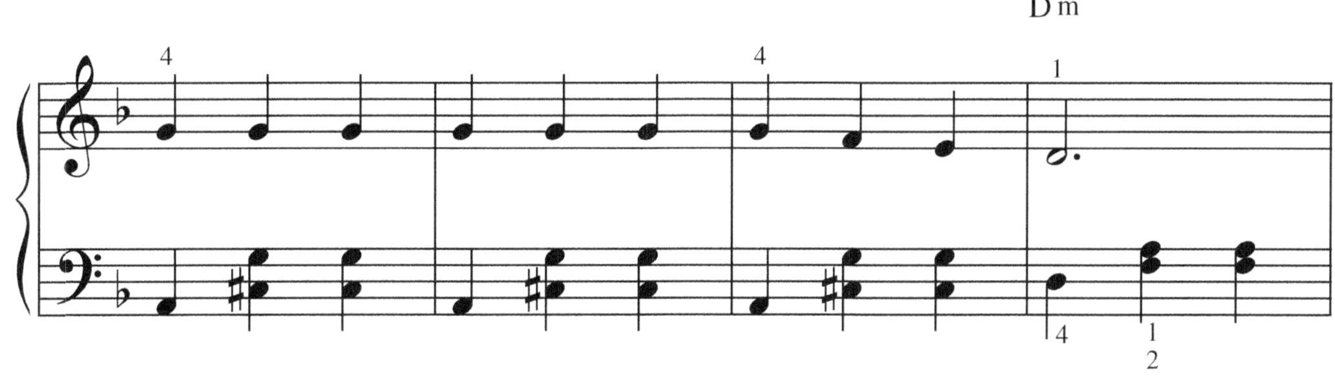

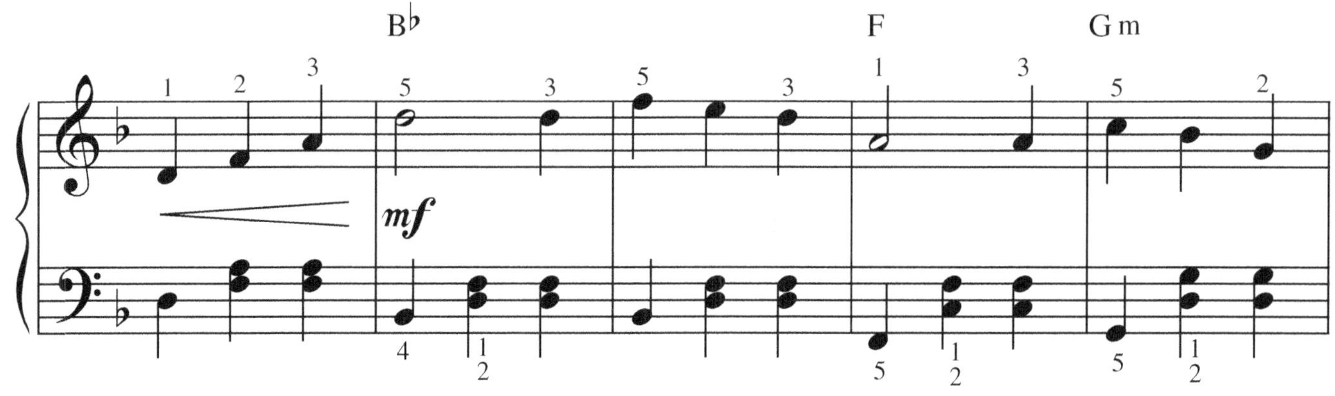

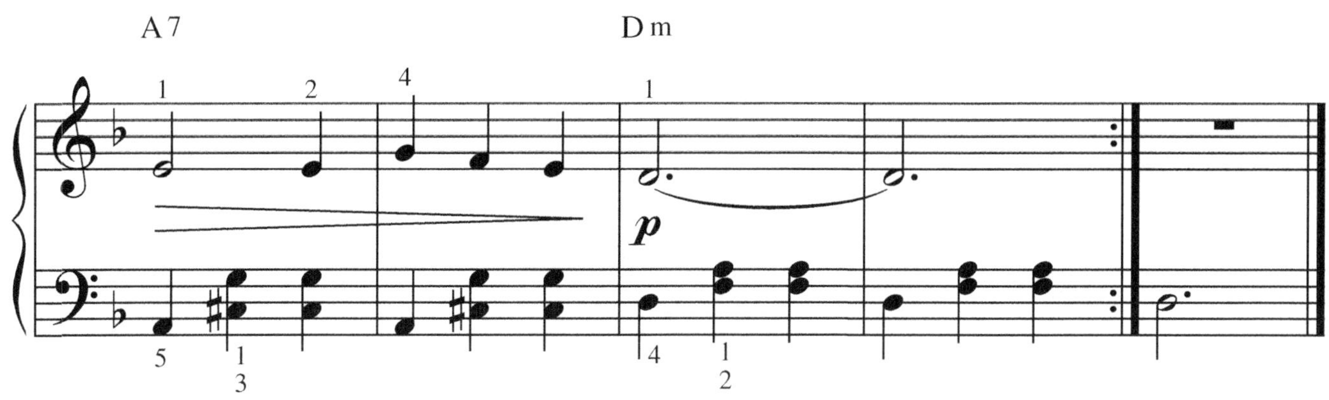

The Rose of Tralee

Ireland (1885)

Unknown composer
Roud 1978
Arr. Bobby Cyr

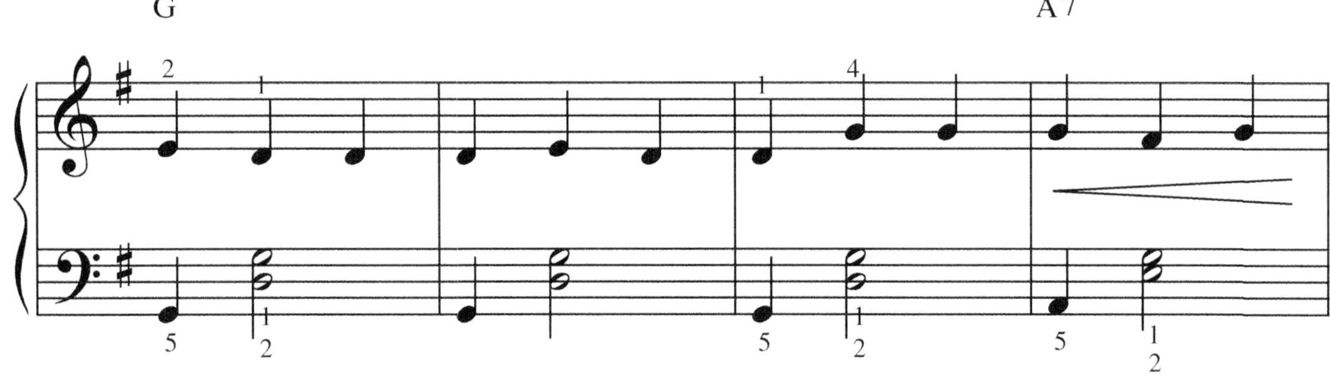

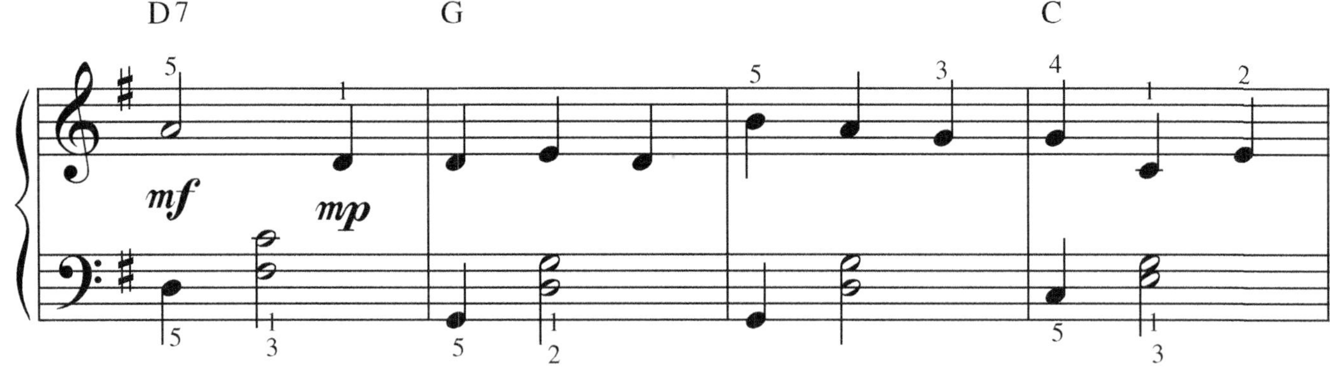

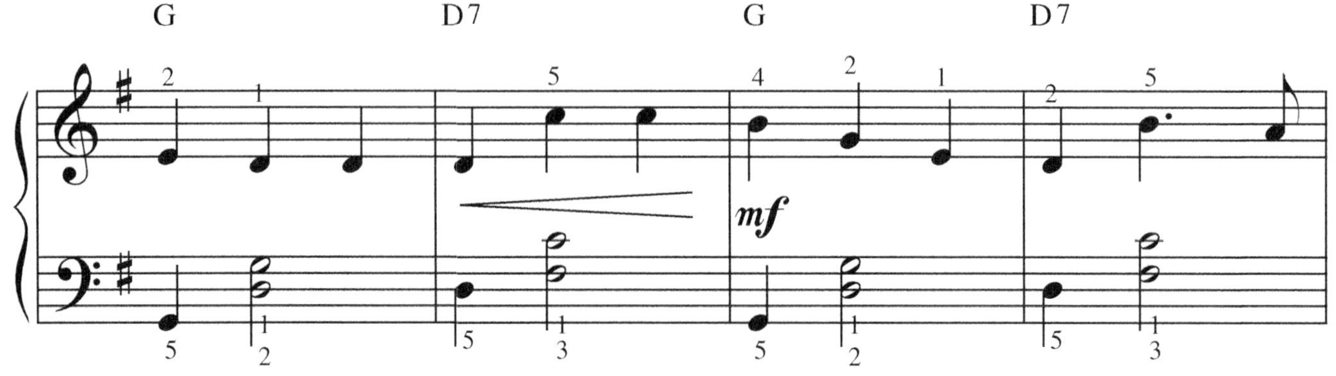

The Rose of Tralee

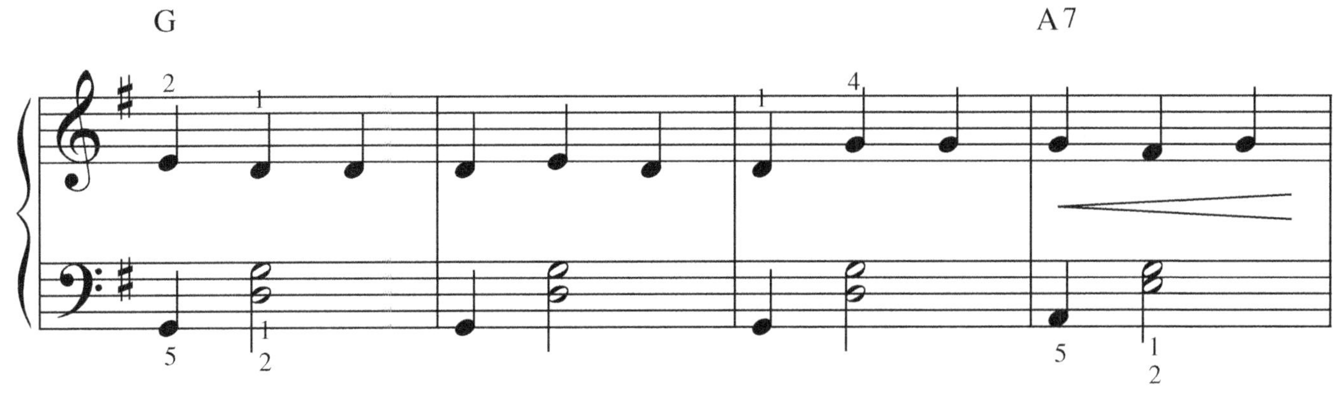

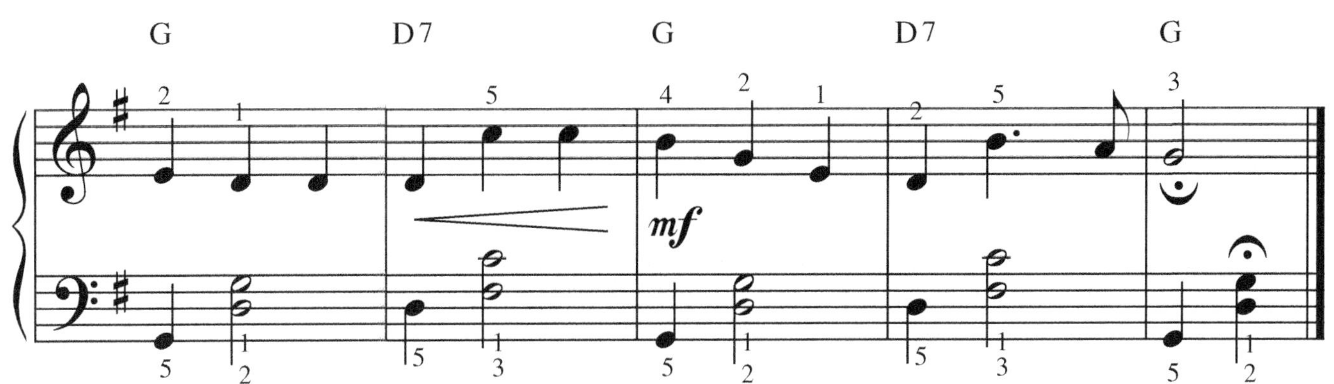

Are You Lonesome Tonight

United States (1926)

Roy Turk
Lou Handman
Arr. Bobby Cyr

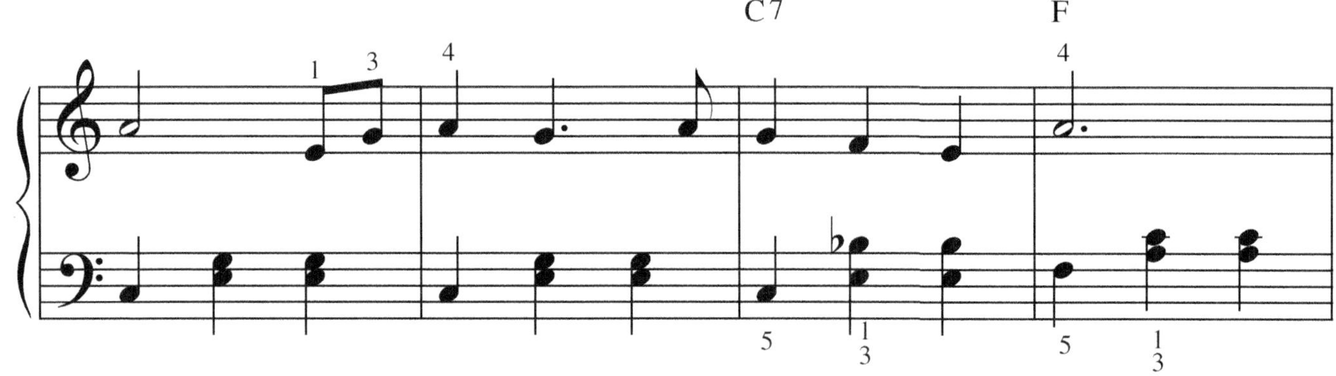

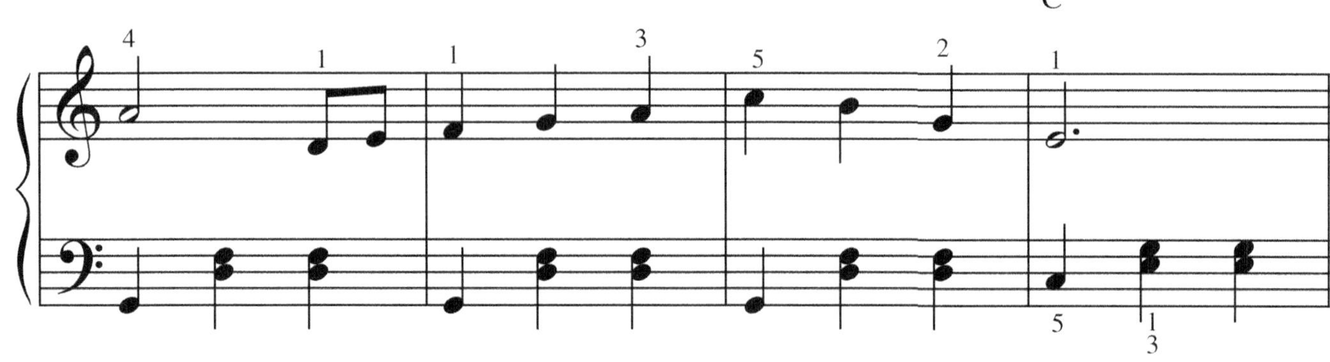

Are You Lonesome Tonight

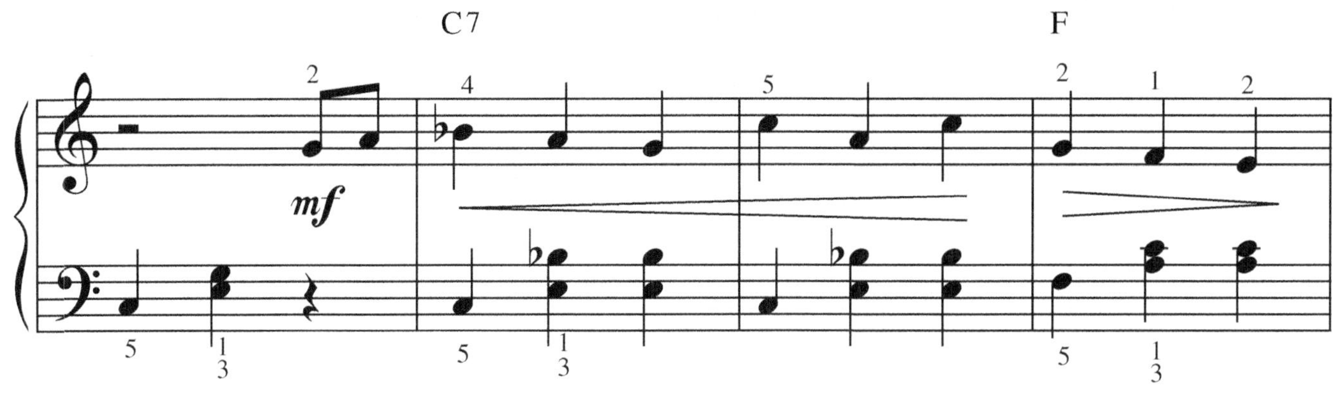

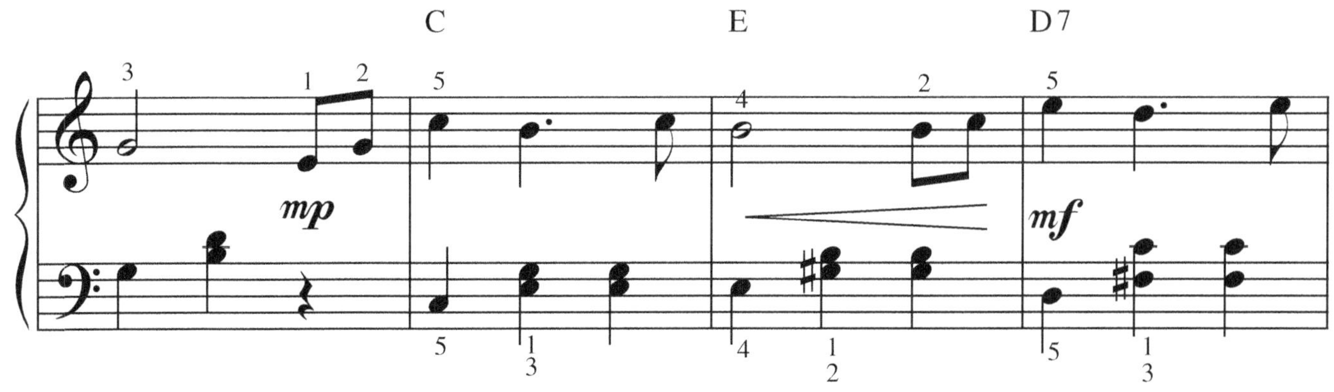

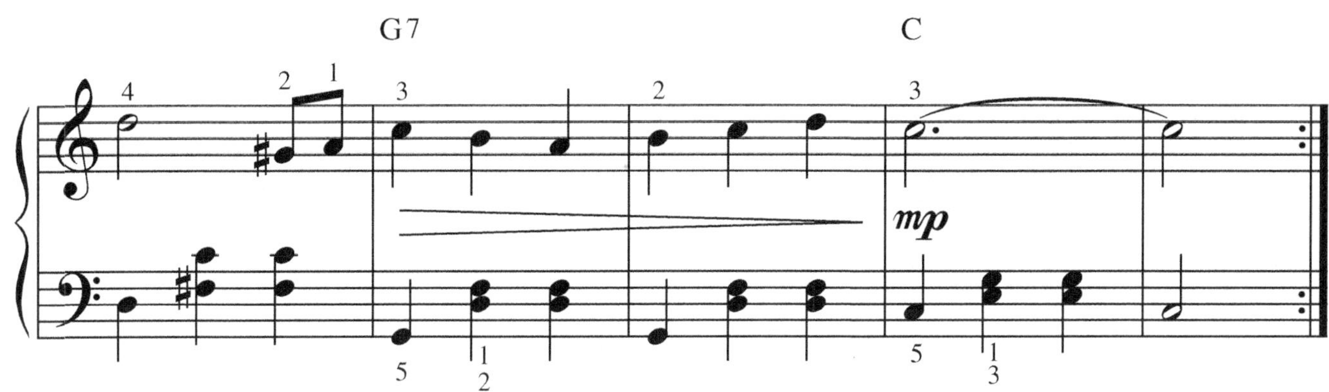

The Entertainer

United States (1902)

Scott Joplin
(1868-1917)
Arr. Bobby Cyr

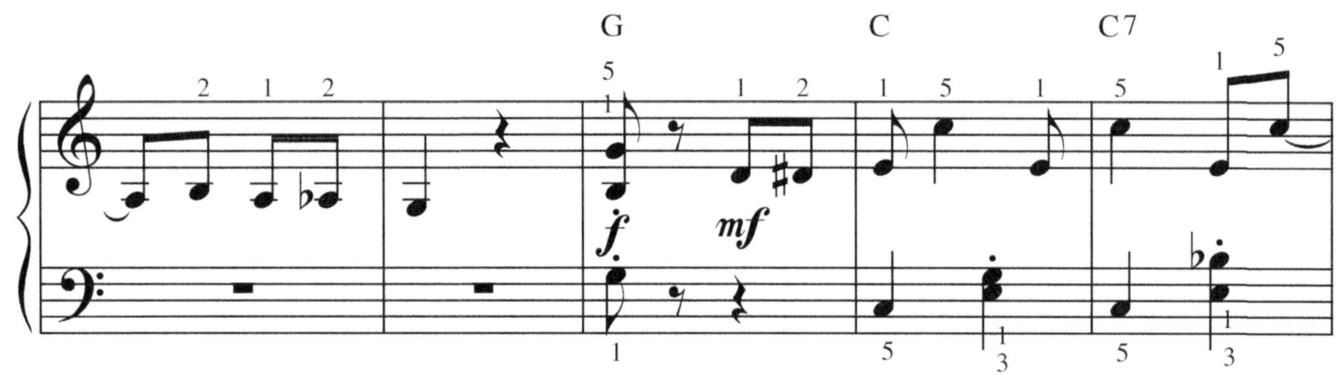

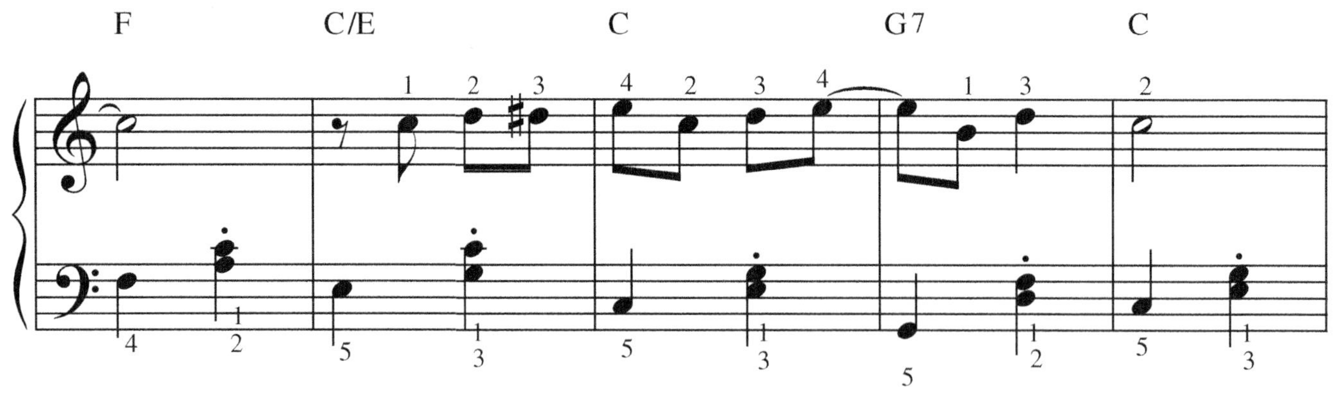

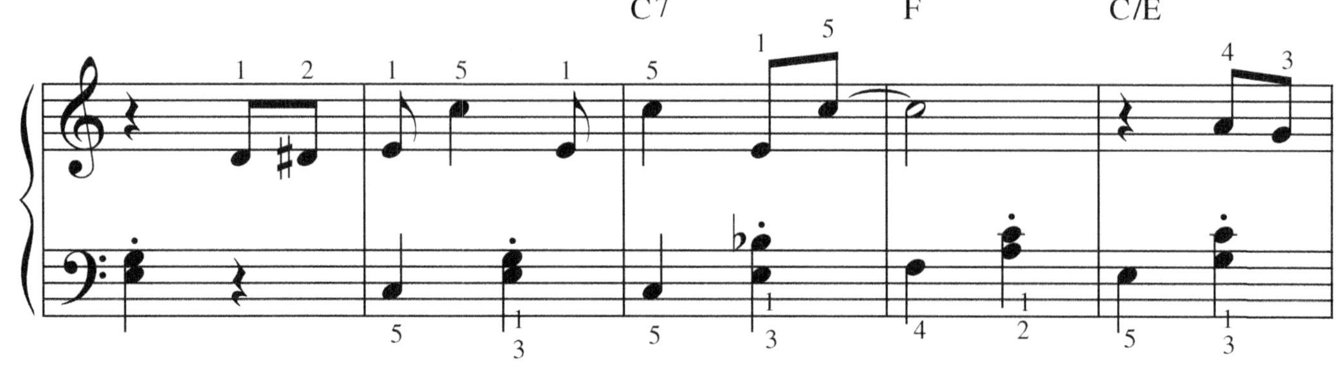

The Entertainer

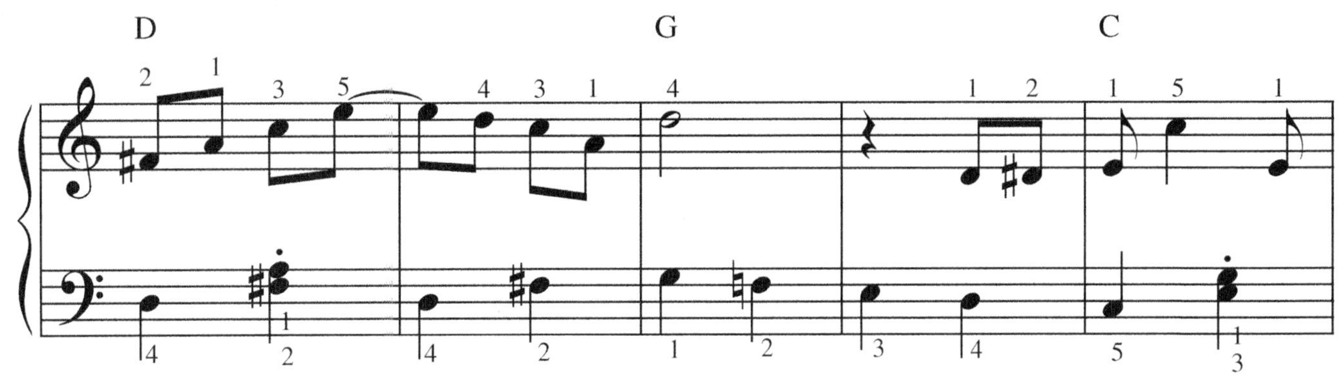

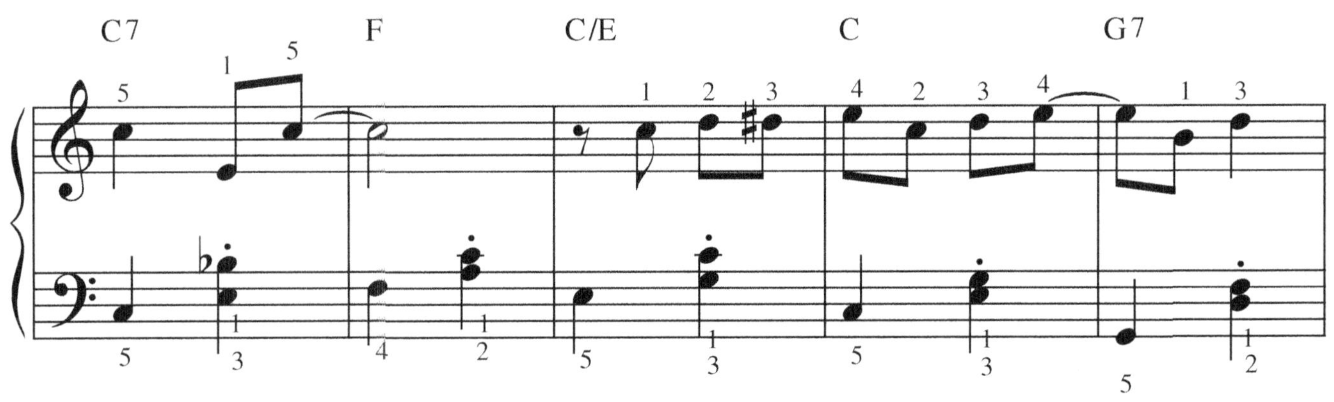

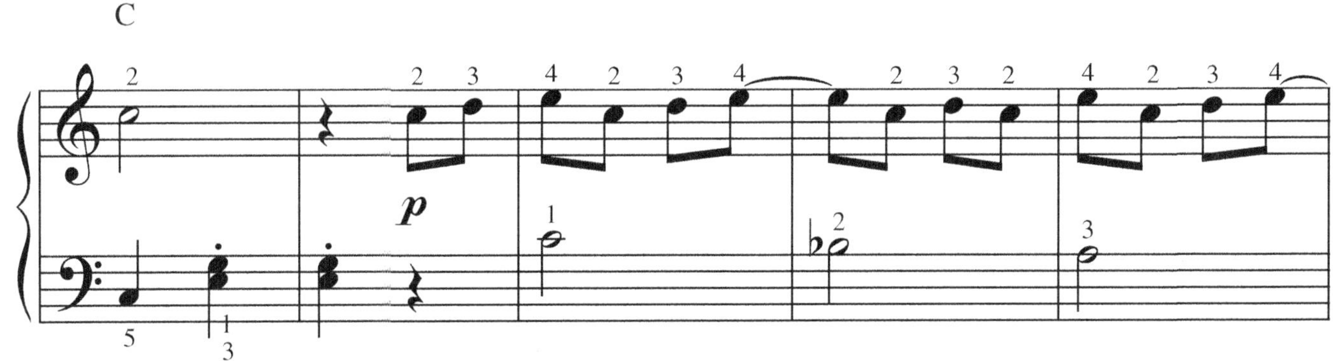

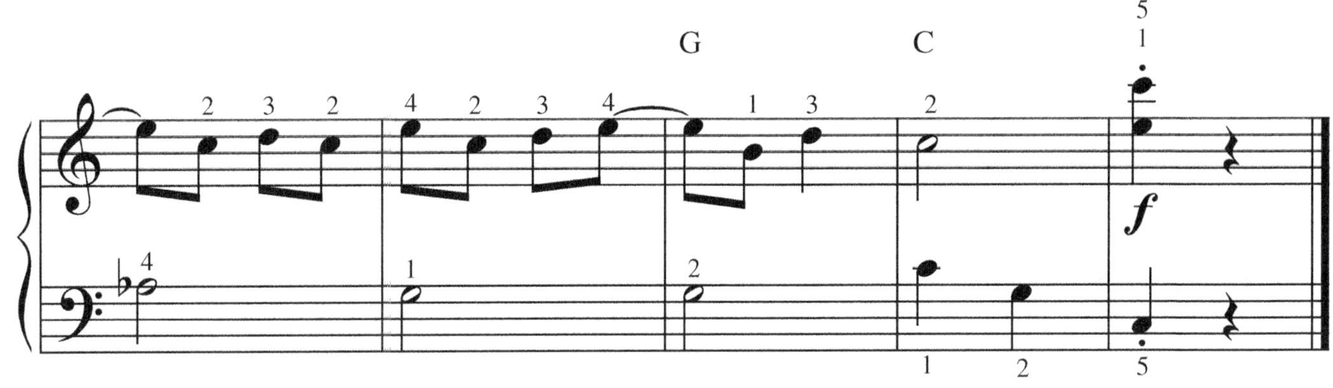

Appendix 1

Concepts for rhythm exercise no. 11

Syncopation

Syncopation occurs when a note is played on a weak beat and held through the following beat.

Count out loud while clapping the rhythm.
Say (and) between each beat.
Then, say (and) silently in your head to master syncopation and offbeats.

Rhythm exercise no. 11 (Syncopation)

Concepts learned in Piano Notion Book Three

Left hand arpeggios

A, Am, Bb, C, D, Dm, E, Em, F, G, Gm,

Seventh chords in the left hand

A7, C7, D7, F7, G7

Chords played with the left hand

Bb, Gm, E, Am/E

Staccato

Syncopation

Certificate of Achievement

This document certifies that

____

Student's name

completed Book Three of the Piano Notion method

On _____________________ _______________________

Date Teacher's name

Congratulations !

Printed in Great Britain
by Amazon

18447525R00052